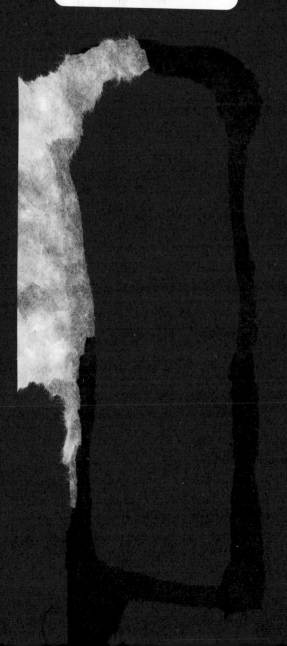

Contents

Jacket: A painting by Costantini
of the assassination of President
Carnot of France by the Italian
anarchist Jeronimo Caserio on
24th June 1894
Front Endpaper: A French cartoon of George V of England
and Nicholas II of Russia threatened by the bombs and daggers
of Anarchists and Nihilists
Rear Endpaper: The cover of a
French songsheet celebrating
the bomb which Vaillant threw into
the Chamber of Deputies

Copyright © 1971: Roderick Kedward
First published in 1971 by
Macdonald Unit 75
St Giles House 49 Poland St London W1
in the British Commonwealth and
American Heritage Press
551 Fifth Avenue New York NY 10017
in the United States of America
Library of Congress Catalogue
Card Number: 75-119459
Made and printed in Great Britain by
Purnell & Sons Ltd Paulton Somerset

THE ANARCHISTS
The men who shocked an era

Roderick Kedward

I should like to thank Mr. David Rumsey of Brighton and M. Maurice Moissonnier of Lyon for documentary material which they kindly provided and I acknowledge a debt owed by all those interested in Anarchism to the books by George Woodcock, James Joll, Gerald Brenan, Paul Avrich and Jean Maitron which are listed on page 126. The Anarchists may be a permanent source of polemic; these studies have made them a permanent subject of history.

H.R.K.   Sussex 1969

American Heritage Press
General Editor: John Roberts

82341

Chapter I
The making of an Anarchist

The great age of the anarchists in Europe and America lay between 1880 and 1914. It was an age which saw the invention of the motor car, moving pictures, and the aeroplane, an age when children discovered they could escape from their parents on bicycles, when, for the first time, thousands of town-dwellers took the train to go sea-bathing, when, as it was said, Edward VII invented the weekend. It was an age of noise, mobility, and the first cheap newspapers. Even the feudal fringe of Europe was affected: Russia, forcefully, and Spain, haphazardly, began to reproduce the signs of urban and industrial growth whose virtues and vices had given the century the dynamism of mass production and the dialectic of the class struggle.

The anarchists were no less dynamic, inventive, and imaginative than their age. Their mobility was a scourge to the police of all countries, their sensational actions stole the headlines of the press and their philosophy of struggle and revolt outstripped all rival doctrines of change. Yet to pursue the similarities any further would be misleading. The anarchists were part of a crowd, but they were figures moving vigorously in the opposite direction.

For if change was accelerated in this period so too was organisation and central control. From social welfare in England to land policy in Russia political and economic life was becoming more organised and centralised, a direction particularly marked in working class politics. Where the 18th century had known spontaneous bread riots by starving labourers and peasant risings in search of land, the end of the 19th century saw the expansion of organised trade unions, socialist parties, and planned revolution.

The anarchists set themselves firmly against this trend. In organisation and centralisation they discerned the principle of authority, a principle to which the word 'anarchy', meaning without government, stood diametrically opposed. For anarchists the root of all evil was govern-

Left: A painting by Flavio Costantini of the assassination of King Umberto of Italy by the anarchist Gaetano Bresci in 1900

5

ment, whether by state, church, party, or individuals. At the door of government they laid the multiple ills of the 19th century, holding it responsible for all inequality and injustice. In 1886 an American anarchist Michael Schwab angrily described the misery of workers in Chicago:

'Thousands of labourers live in rooms without sufficient protection from the weather, without proper ventilation, where never a stream of sunlight flows in. There are hovels where two, three, or four families live in one room. . . . And how do they live? From the dustbins they gather half-rotten vegetables, in the butchers' shops they buy for some cents offal of meat, and these precious morsels they carry home to prepare from them their meals. Is it not horrible in a so-called civilised land where there is plenty of food and riches?'

The place was Chicago, but it could have been London, Paris, or Turin, or with some adaptation the peasant villages of Andalusia in Spain or Siberia in Russia. The existence of extreme poverty was the undercurrent of a society which vaunted its ideas of progress, its technological inventions, and its material gains.

The rulers of such a society, proclaimed the anarchists, were guilty of intolerable hypocrisy and their authority was a violent assault on human freedom. Inequality, they stated, was a direct product of authority as churchgoers themselves contentedly sang:

'The rich man in his castle
The poor man at his gate
God made them high and lowly
And ordered their estate.'

It was just this sentiment which the anarchists indignantly rejected. The only way to equality and justice they believed was to destroy all traces of authority and to build a society without government in which man would be free to create the happiness of which he was capable.

This was the bond that united all anarchists: antagonism to any situation regulated by imposition, constraint, or oppression. Beyond this the anarchists produced a wealth of disagreement. No single coherent programme of anarchism emerged: dispute and discord were of its very nature. It remaind a collection of different emotions, ideas, and actions, a broken mosaic of richly coloured pieces.

How should authority be destroyed? How would the great change in society be accomplished? What kind of action would bring about the ideal life of anarchy? Anarchism from its start is a history of partial answers to these questions.

Right: *'The master of us all' — Pierre-Joseph Proudhon, one of the great theorists of anarchism, painted by Gustave Courbet*

The prophets of revolution

For Michael Bakunin (1814-76), the giant among early anarchists, the answer was instant revolution by all the underprivileged, whether peasants, industrial workers, unemployed intellectuals, or discontented students. Seen by Wagner as a destroyer of the Gods, Bakunin, massive in physique, voracious in appetite, played a leading role in five attempted revolutions throughout Europe, all of which were either failures or tragi-comedies. His efforts to create an international revolutionary movement also came to nothing: the Marxian socialists rejected his anarchist solutions and his own anarchist followers were too diffuse to sustain an international movement. He died a lonely and unsuccessful figure but the shadow of his great unaccomplished revolution had passed over most of Europe and the myths and ideals lived on.

For his older contemporary, Pierre Joseph Proudhon (1809-65), described by Bakunin as the 'master of us all', the anarchist answer was an economic one. The two great values in life, he believed, were justice and work and he envisaged a society of independent economic groups in which all men were to do a just share of work to produce the food and goods necessary for a contented and un-ambitious life. Proudhon was by trade a printer and the craftsman's mentality was a determinant in his anarchist thinking. His economic groups were reminiscent of medieval craft guilds and although he had inside experi-ence of revolution among Parisian workers in 1848 he never provided a blueprint for an urban, industrialised anarchism, nor a clear theory of how an increasingly in-terdependent economy was to be broken down into the autonomous units which he described. For this reason his influence was strongest among artisans or in countries with a non-industrialised economy. Indian anarchists in the 20th century, for example, have found his ideas both relevant and practical.

Bakunin and Proudhon provided the first two proto-types of anarchist action: revolution which would destroy and create in one cataclysmic movement of popular insur-rection, and economic independence to allow working men to gain an equal and just reward for their productive labour. Capitalism, government, and property would be the victims and the poor would inherit the earth.

Between 1848 and 1880 anarchist ideas and practices were moulded on one or other of these two prototypes or

Left: Mass poverty and the squalid conditions created by industrialisation and rapid increases in population (top right and bottom) were the breeding ground for anarchism. Many emigrants who fled to America (top left) were to find that conditions there were little better than those they had left

Les Hommes du jour

PUBLICATION HEBDOMADAIRE PARAISSANT LE SAMEDI

Dessin de A. Delannoy   Texte de Flax

Pierre KROPOTKINE

on a mixture of both, though local leaders, such as the schoolmaster James Guillaume who inspired the anarchist federation of Swiss watchmakers and peasants in the Jura, were careful not to become Bakuninists or Proudhonists in any slavish sense. After 1880, however, Bakunin and Proudhon, the pioneers of anarchist action, became only two among the multiple sources of anarchist belief and method.

In the realm of theory Peter Kropotkin (1842-1921), Russian prince and eminent geographer, was the most fertile intellectual source at the end of the century. His mixture of anarchism and communism, whether expressed amid the horror of Siberian working conditions or from the respectability of suburban London, stressed the need for co-operation as the working principle of anarchist action. He welcomed any institution based on a spirit of voluntary co-operation and equality. By co-operation, he believed, society could be transformed into a civilisation far higher than that reached by struggle and conflict, the twin obsessions of those who were adapting Darwin's 'struggle for survival' to fit the world of social behaviour. With such a belief Kropotkin's writings are a landmark in human optimism, though at the same time they drew a bitter and savage picture of social corruption and disillusionment:

'You, young engineer [he wrote in an *Appeal to the Young* in 1885] who dream of bettering the lot of workers by applying the inventions of science to industry, what a sad disenchantment, what deceptions await you. You devote the youthful energy of your intellect to working out the plan of some railway, which, winding round the edges of precipices and piercing the heart of huge mountains, will unite two countries separated by nature. But when once the work is on foot you see whole regiments of workers decimated by privations and sickness in this gloomy tunnel, you see others returning home taking with them a few pence and the seeds of consumption, you see each yard of the line marked off by human corpses, the result of grovelling greed; and finally, when the line is at last opened, you see it used as a highway for the artillery of an invading army.'

Was co-operation the best way to fight this picture of exploitation? To many anarchists Kropotkin's remedy appeared too intellectual, too utopian: they responded more readily when, in strange contradiction to his own gentle nature, he called for 'permanent revolt by word of mouth, in writing, by the dagger, the rifle, dynamite.

Far Left: The other giants of anarchism—Michael Bakunin (bottom), and Prince Peter Kropotkin (top). Left: A slum in Glasgow—a scene common to all 19th-century industrial states

11

... Everything is good for us which falls outside legality'. In no sense was Kropotkin a violent man, yet he could not dissociate himself from the revolutionary tradition of anarchism much as he preferred a more passive solution. His call to revolt, therefore, became as celebrated as his appeal for co-operation.

'Go murder, pray, and die'

In fact no such call was needed. Throughout Europe and America anarchists were discovering the possibilities of violence, without recourse to the writings of Kropotkin or any other theorist. Violence in the late 19th century became the most spontaneous and dramatic of the anarchists' answers: society was to be transformed by assassination, bombs, and individual acts of terrorism. In the public mind the word anarchy rapidly became synonymous with this violence and in 1901 the words of President Theodore Roosevelt summed up the reputation gained by anarchists in two decades of terror. 'Anarchism is a crime against the whole human race and all mankind should band against the anarchists.'

Both in these words and in general public opinion, the anarchists who killed President Carnot of France, Empress Elizabeth of Austria, policemen of all countries, President McKinley of America, and a number of theatregoers, café clientèle, and a wide range of others, were held clearly responsible for initiating violence. The anarchists themselves returned the accusation, accusing government, church, capital, and property of ruling by violence and claiming that their own violence was no more than the individual's right to self-defence. History, they argued, was a pageant of violence sanctioned by authority. In mockery they sang:

'Onward Christian soldiers! Duty's way is plain,
Slay your Christian neighbours or by them be slain.
Pulpiteers are spouting effervescent swill,
God above is calling you to rob and rape and kill.
All your acts are sanctified by the Lamb on high
If you love the Holy Ghost, go murder, pray, and die.'

The aggression of this parody was typical of a climate of violence. There is little doubt that an anarchist like Ravachol, whose bombs terrified Paris in 1892, believed that his actions were defensive, but they added to a spiral of public and private violence which brought more power to police, army, and government and in no way undermined authority. As a means to achieve the ideal society

Left: One of the spectacular attacks on political leaders which gained anarchism such notoriety—a contemporary impression of the assassination of President Carnot of France by the Italian anarchist Jeronimo Caserio in 24th June 1894

it was hotly debated among anarchists themselves and the terrorists were seen to be marginal figures, isolated on the fringe of the anarchist movements.

But not surprisingly, the violence captured and kept the headlines and as a result little public justice was done to two other anarchist positions which emerged at the turn of the century. The first was an uncompromising individualism and the second an equally assertive syndicalism, or trade-unionism.

Belief that the individual, free from external pressures and traditional prejudice, could live a happy enlightened life is not limited to anarchism. However disguised, it is one of the most persistent themes in the history of Western thought inspiring a succession of innovators, ascetics, and unorthodox rebels. Like Kropotkin's belief in co-operation it is basically optimistic, rejecting those discoveries which show the individual to be little more than an animal or little less than a machine. The key word again is freedom, and for this reason individualism is represented in most anarchist thought and practice from Bakunin to the anarchist students in the Parisian revolution of May 1968. Its zenith, however, was reached in the two decades before 1914, when individual self-assertion was rife throughout society, particularly in the arts.

The anarchist individualists adopted a little-known German writer, Max Stirner, as their prophet. Stirner (1806-56), the pseudonym of Johann Caspar Schmidt, was apparently a mild, inoffensive schoolteacher who shocked the school where he was teaching, a Berlin academy for young ladies, by producing a book calling for complete individualism, the assertive dominance of the self. To be 'oneself' at the expense of state, family, or merely 'others' was for Stirner, the highest good, and in pursuit of this egoism he justified any action, rebellion and crime included. Of little importance in his day, the gentle Herr Schmidt was rediscovered at the end of the century and, as Max Stirner, he became a powerful incitement to individualist action.

Above all, this individualism meant putting anarchist ideas immediately into practice and not waiting for society to change. Those who rejected marriage lived with any partner of their choice or set up free love communities; those who rejected war refused military service; those who rejected the laws of society lived outside them; those women who believed in female emancipation took men's jobs and practised birth control. The purpose was to be morally independent and to think for oneself, ration-

Right: The arrest of Ravachol whose bomb attacks in 1892 made him one of the most notorious and widely-discussed anarchists

14

ally and without prejudice. In 1908 one pamphleteer and lecturer in France, Paraf-Javal, defined anarchism so narrowly in terms of independent, rational thought that he concluded:

'The majority of individuals of our age who call themselves anarchists are almost all more ignorant, more dirty, and more pathological than those whom they call bourgeois: they are often alcoholics, tobacco addicts, and megalomaniacs. Only those anarchists who think rationally and scientifically are true anarchists.'

The definition in no way covers the complexity of anarchism. What it does is to illustrate anarchist individualism: no mention of economics, politics, or class, the stress is purely of an attitude of mind.

By contrast anarchist trade unionism, known as anarcho-syndicalism, was forged in the heat of economic protest and class division. Starting in France in the 1890s, it was a significant departure in anarchist history. A departure because no earlier form of anarchism had adapted itself to industrial action, and significant because it produced in the Spanish trade union Federation, the *Confederacion Nacional del Trabajo* (CNT), the most effective anarchist movement in modern Europe. Essentially, anarcho-syndicalism aimed to transform society by means of strikes, in particular the general strike, mounted as a revolutionary action by all workers and ushering in the age of freedom and justice. From economic chaos, from the ashes of capitalism would rise the phoenix of anarchy. With such an ideal it stood as the economic twin to Bakunin's political revolution, but it also produced offshoots of a more pragmatic nature: labour exchanges, classes for workers' education, and hard-headed wage claims. Above all it kept itself independent of party politics, scornful of both liberal democracy and parliamentary socialism, both of which were seen as playing the bourgeois game of political authority.

In the CNT anarchism appeared to achieve a viable compromise between organisation and freedom, something which other forms of anarchism felt to be unworthy or unnecessary. Of all the anarchist visions of change, anarcho-syndicalism was the only one to offer a glimpse of success. In general the problem of how to destroy authority and leave freedom behind remained a tantalus situation; the answer was often in sight but always out of reach. In fact anarchism as we know it would have lost much of its vital character had it reached and caught hold of an answer. It fed on the belief and promise **21** ▷

Far left: Two covers of 'L'Almanach du Pere Reinard', the most widely-read and scurilous French anarchist magazine. Left: French troops and police after a battle with anarchists

'A crime against the human race'

To the increasingly prosperous middle-classes at the end of the 19th century, the Anarchists seemed especially sinister and horrifying. Not only did their random violence—the bombs in theatres and cafés—seem senseless acts which threatened innocent individuals; but their whole philosophy was an assault upon the assumptions and institutions which held up the established order. It was therefore natural that magazines and newspapers should vie with each other in printing lurid and sensational accounts of anarchist activities; and that the sinister anarchist with his bomb should become a popular bogeyman and part of subsequent mythology. **Right:** A page from the *Illustrated London News* giving a blow by blow account of the tracking down and arrest of anarchists involved in an explosion at Greenwich. Joseph Conrad based his book *The Secret Agent* on this event. **Below:** A typical impression of the enemy of humanity at work making bombs in his laboratory

THE SCENE OUTSIDE THE GR

SERGEANT MICHAEL WALSH, IN W

SEARCHING THE POCKETS OF

ATORY: THE FINDING OF BOURDIN AFTER
OSION

ABOUT NINE O'CLOCK, WHEN LEAST CROWDED, THE POLICE, IN PLAIN CLOTHES, ARRIVED
AND TOOK POSSESSION OF THE CLUB AUTONOMIE, IN WINDMILL STREET

ARY DOORKEEPER, USHERED THE MEMBERS
THIS WAY, PLEASE "

EVERY NOOK AND CRANNY OF THE CLUB WAS INVESTIGATED WITH DARK
LANTERNS FOR INCRIMINATING DOCUMENTS

ANARCHISTS

ALL THE MEN WHOM CHIEF INSPECTOR MELVILLE SUSPECTED WERE TAKEN INTO THE BAR OF THE CLUB AND
CLOSELY INTERROGATED

L'ESPRIT DE RÉVOLTE

Prix : 0,10

LE SALARIAT

that Truth, Justice, and Freedom would be established and that a New World of Liberty would replace the Old World of Oppression. While these ideals lay in the future, while they were still unrealised, their power to inspire and impassion was unlimited. For this reason anarchists can be seen as men working towards a millenium, the reign of anarchy on earth. To an unbelieving world the anarchists proclaimed what they saw as the one undying right of all humanity, the freedom of man's mind and body. In 1886, concluding his speech to the court which condemned him to death, the American anarchist August Spies declared:

'If you think you can crush out these ideas that are gaining ground more and more every day, if you think you can crush them out by sending us to the gallows, if you would once more have people suffer the penalty of death because they have dared tell the truth, I say if death is the penalty for proclaiming the truth then I will proudly and defiantly pay the costly price. Call your hangman! Truth crucified in Socrates, Christ, Giordano Bruno, in Huss, in Galileo still lives. They and others whose number is legion have preceded us. We are ready to follow!'

The mark of the anarchist was this certainty that anarchism was truth and that truth would in the end triumph.

The myth of Ravachol

But who *were* the anarchists? What kind of people were they? What were their jobs, their situations in society? These questions were first seriously asked in the mid-1890s at the height of anarchist violence and one anarchist in particular was the subject of intensive discussion. His name was François Königstein but he was known as Ravachol. On 11th March 1892 in the heart of Paris a bomb had exploded on the staircase of 136 Boulevard St Germain. On 27th March another exploded in a building in the Rue de Clichy. Three days later Ravachol, responsible for both explosions, was overpowered by ten policemen in the Boulevard Magenta.

The public soon knew that Ravachol had a long history of theft and forgery, that he had disinterred a corpse in search of jewels, and murdered an old hermit before stealing his horde of money. Brought before two courts, Ravachol was condemned to death for the murder, and on 11th July the guillotine interrupted his last cry of defiance, 'Vive la Ré . . .' which the police interpreted optimistically as 'Long live the Republic', but which was almost certainly a final call to Revolution. At his death he was

Far left: 'Permanent revolt by word.' The major theoretical foundation of anarchism, the covers of two of Kropotkin's books. Left: French workers returning from a strike meeting at Meru

21

significantly thirty-three: in Spain an uncle of the anarchist Salvador had blown out his brains at the same age exclaiming 'Christ only lived to thirty-three. Why should I live longer?' and Salvador himself was thirty-three when he threw a bomb into a theatre killing twenty people.

In such way myths are born and Ravachol entered at once into anarchist legend. Songs were composed to celebrate his actions and sung at down-at-heel cafés in the depressed quarters of Paris, and his proud self-justification at his trial and his indifference to execution made his death into something of a martyrdom. He was by no means the first terrorist but his combination of anarchist ideals and flamboyant terror seized the public imagination in a new way and his strange and brutal history attracted the attention of experts in all fields. Sociologists, priests, lawyers, doctors, and others began to produce explanations and descriptions of anarchism, and in 1894 came the first major attempt to place Ravachol and his fellow terrorists into categories, the work of a criminologist, the famous Cesare Lombroso of Italy.

Lombroso divided anarchists into types, one of which he called the 'born criminal', a man whose physical features were held to betray his criminal tendencies. Ravachol is given as a perfect example – 'brutal, asymmetric face, with exaggerated nostrils, nose twisted to the right, ears like handles at different heights and a huge lower jaw, square and dominating', a portrait very different from the romantic photograph by which Ravachol is normally remembered. Anarchism, Lombroso stated, was full of such criminal faces. Out of forty-one anarchists in Paris he found 31 per cent with a criminal physiognomy: in Chicago 40 per cent of forty-three and in Turin 34 per cent of a hundred, whereas among members of other extremist movements he found percentages of only 6 per cent and 12 per cent. One sign of natural criminality among anarchists, he continued, was the habit of tatooing. On several anarchists he had seen anchors, hearts, and crossbows and even 'I love you' in English.

Not all Lombroso's observations are as bizarre as these: he had a shrewd understanding of the injustices of society which encouraged the spirit of anarchist revolt, but his account of the criminal type among anarchists was both influential and typical of the period. By 1900 it was widely presumed that most anarchists were of this type and, being criminals, should be treated as such.

Subsequent historians of anarchism have often dealt with the terrorists in much the same way, labelling them

Right: A Punch cartoon which shows how seriously anarchism was regarded as an attack on the fabric of contemporary society

as criminals, fanatics, or psychopaths and diverting the reader's attention to other anarchists of a more praiseworthy nature. But, although it is true that terrorists were not at the centre of anarchist history, their mentality and background reveal two factors which many other anarchists also had in common. In the first place most of the terrorists were products of social, economic, or personal misery and secondly most of them were solitary figures determined to preserve their independence.

Ravachol himself was the son of unmarried parents; his father frequently beat his mother before finally leaving her in poverty with four children. The young boy was then brought up in an institution and by the age of eight was in employment as a farm labourer herding cows and goats. He had to beg for money and clothes, and his pattern of life became a succession of jobs, interwoven with periods of acute poverty. Deprived of affection throughout his childhood, he became aggressive and mistrustful, and his character adapted easily to the idea of violence both in the service of anarchism and crime.

Among the anarchist assassins one can see the same deprivation and solitude. The Italian assassin, Luigi Luccheni, was left by his mother in a poor house in Parma. By the age of nine he was working on the Italian railways, before beginning a rapid sequence of jobs which left him embittered against all employers and figures of authority. Isolated and unsuccessful he dreamed of making his name by a sensational act. 'I'd like to kill somebody,' he said, 'but it must be someone important so that it gets into the papers.' On 10th September 1898, he stabbed to death the Empress Elizabeth of Austria, a tragic figure who wrote sad, romantic poetry and had nothing to do with politics.

Case studies throughout the world of anarchism show the persistence of these two factors, social misery and assertive independence, which were prominent in the lives of Ravachol and Luccheni. More was needed to produce a violent personality, but these two factors in combination frequently explain the making of an anarchist, and independence by itself is the most recurrent characteristic in the psychology and sociology of anarchism. In particular, it was thoroughly entrenched in the two social groups which formed the backbone of anarchism; artisans and poor peasants.

Both groups were threatened by more efficient competitors, by the advent of industry and mechanisation and by the periodic economic depressions which only the bigger

Top: A bomb of the type used by Henry in his attack on the Café Terminus (left). The damage caused by Ravachol's bomb in the Rue de Clichy (right). Bottom: A wagon specially designed by the Paris police for removing unexploded anarchist bombs

82341

producers could survive. In the face of these threats, they tended to fall back on the very quality which was keeping them in the backwater of economic development, their independence. It was part of the psychology of 19th-century artisans that they often preferred to be independent, even though poor, rather than members of a wage-earning labour force, and of the peasants that they often chose to remain on their own small, unproductive piece of land rather than become landless agricultural labourers. Both the capitalists and the marxists labelled this determined independence as backward-looking or reactionary and neither the modernising industrial state nor the socialist proletariat had time or sympathy for the artisan and peasant. Anarchism on the other hand offered a defence of their freedom and a right to live and work in their own ways.

In Lyons in 1894 out of 152 anarchists in the police files, 55 per cent were artisans, including thirty-nine shoemakers, sixteen weavers, eleven plasterers and eight dyers. Among the rest there was only a handful of wage-earning industrial workers. In the 1870s in the pioneer anarchist societies of the Swiss Jura, the militants were mostly watchmakers, working individually in their own homes, while in the 1900s in the East End of London Rudolf Rocker, an immigrant German bookbinder found the world of Jewish tailors and other artisans receptive to his anarchist teaching.

The rise of peasant anarchism
Poor peasants, particularly in Spain and Russia, present a parallel case. In the Ukraine the famous anarchist Nestor Makhno who became a guerrilla chieftain in the Russian Civil War was a peasant, with peasant followers, and in Spain smallholders provided the tenacious anarchist leaders in the Andalusian villages. Their standard of living was at best a little above starvation level and anarchist revolts like the march on Jerez in 1892 occurred usually in the bleak winter months when hunger was at its peak. In the villages the Spanish government was represented by the Civil Guard, whose armed excursions into the country to repress any signs of rebellion or banditry were a constant reminder to the peasants of authoritarian control. The anarchism that developed there aimed at the total removal of this hated outside authority and Bakunin's ideal of a great Revolution was held in almost mystical veneration.

In France the phenomenon of peasant anarchism was rare and in fact several early commentators attributed the rise of anarchism to the nefarious influence of the towns. In 1895 a doctor and magistrate Dr Charles Calmeilles, who was mayor of a small country town described the

making of an anarchist in these words:

'If, reaching the town, a country boy receives an education far above his social position; if, leaving the fields, he throws himself into studies ruinous for his family and finds his efforts useless to keep him, what do you expect? He lives by expediency from day to day, he blames society for all his ills, he joins those gangrenous circles where vice and evil ideas flourish, he creates harmful relationships and soon begins to dream of total destruction. Anarchist theories attract him and may become his own, and this boy who would have made an honest man, a solid worker with strong arms, who would have married a beautiful country girl, a flower of the field, by whom he would have had the kind of healthy, robust children who are the might and fortune of France, this boy remains a good-for-nothing, and worse than that becomes a fervent disciple of evil.'

The remedy, the doctor continues, is the compulsory return of all anarchists to the village soil.

Clearly Dr Calmeilles knew nothing of peasant anarchism but his account is not worthless for all its bucolic self-confidence. By his description he illustrates a social group from which many anarchists came, a group made up of students and intellectuals from the universities who lived a precarious hand to mouth existence.

Students in the 19th century were not just the sons of the privileged who took up places at the leading universities as part of their social inheritance. They were also those whose intelligence gained them recognition but whose lack of money or status made the completion of their courses either impossible or extremely debilitating. There is nothing mythical about the starving student in his garret and Puccini's *La Bohème*, freed from its nostalgia, can be seen as a piece of realism. Many students spent most of their time finding money to live and their situation was in no way assured at the end of their studies. In Russia universities were used as a step to the Civil Service but often the poor student would rise no higher than a badly paid clerk if he had not been dismissed long before for expressing liberal ideas. In 1884 a Tsarist statute dissolved university clubs and societies, banished liberal professors to obscure parts of Russia, and destroyed all university autonomy. The students bitterly resented the constant intrusion of authority and in the

*Left: Lombroso, the Italian criminologist **(top left)**, with some of his 'criminal types': Ravachol **(upper centre left)**, Vaillant **(lower centre left)**, Caserio **(bottom left)**, Czolgocz **(top right)**, and three of the Russian anarchists who took part in the attempts to assassinate Tsar Alexander II, Sophie Perovskaya **(upper centre right)**, Chalturin **(lower centre right)**, and Balmaschov **(bottom right)***

27

biggest Russian anarchist group *Chernoe Zhania* (Black Banner) students played a leading role, the average age of the movement being little more than twenty. In Italy Andrea Costa started as a student anarchist at Bologna before moving in the 1880s into constitutional socialism, and Bakunin, on his visits to Italy, had placed high hopes on the dissident intelligentsia which proliferated in the university towns.

The students who responded to anarchism did so not just because they were poor or unemployed, but also because they despaired of piecemeal reform in society and demanded solutions which were total and uncompromising. They despised Marxist students and intellectuals whose arguments seemed to them over subtle and academic and because, like artisans, they were often solitary figures, they rejected the answers of organised trade unions and political parties. Their preference in Russia was expressed in the slogan of a St Petersburg anarchist group 'mighty and ruthless, total and bloody, people's vengeance'. It was a violent, primitive emotion, intellectually satisfying to those who saw absolute revolt as the only answer to the Tsar's absolute authority.

To say that anarchists were to be found among artisans, poor peasants, and students is not to say that these groups invariably produced anarchists or that anarchists invariably came from these groups. In no class or economic grouping, outside Spain, was anarchism the norm. Even among artisans and peasants anarchism never became a representative creed: only among the Spanish workers of the CNT did it achieve this position. Internationally the anarchists could never claim to speak for a recognised class or group interest and in this lay both their weakness and their strength. Without a solid class backing they were powerless, yet their support for 'all victims of authority' gave them a moral strength which appeared to transcend narrower class interests. Anarchists, it has even been stated, were anarchists because they had no class consciousness.

In fact many of the more prominent anarchists came from outside the labouring and deprived classes of society altogether. They were members of aristocratic or gentry families who embraced anarchist ideas in revolt against their own background and the values of a hierarchical society. Bakunin and Kropotkin were both sons of the Russian aristocracy while the Italian leader Carlo Cafiero came from a rich family and Errico Malatesta, according to various interpretations, from one that was wealthy or moderately wealthy.

The drive which took these scions of privilege into the

Right: *Errico Malatesta photographed while in exile in London*

ranks of anarchism cannot be assessed in social terms, and certainly not in terms of class or economic grouping. Philanthropy was the time-honoured way for the wealthy to express their sympathy for the lower classes and Malatesta, for example, might well have stopped at this point when he worked among cholera victims in Naples. Kropotkin equally might have been satisfied with the pity he showed as a young officer to the convicts in the Siberian gold mines. But Malatesta left the society of his parents, started work as an electrician, and began assiduously to plan for anarchist revolution while Kropotkin rejected his safe career in the Tsarist army and dedicated himself first to geographic research and finally to anarchist propaganda by word and deed. Both knew what authority meant and both came to see it as evil and oppressive. Kropotkin, as a result of his experience in the army, also saw it as corrupt and inefficient. Their anarchism was a personal and intellectual revolt: they acted as individuals, not as representatives of their class.

In the 1930s the English poet and art critic Herbert Read appeared to cater for the rebellious aristocrat when he declared, with a nod towards Freud, 'I would define the anarchist as the man who in his manhood dares to resist the authority of the father.' Bakunin, in fact, ascribed his restless, revolutionary nature to his resistance against a tyrannical mother and other anarchists were clearly reacting against authority figures outside the family, such as employers, police, or statesmen. There were also those who rejected God and the Church after an early life of religious devotion. Marked by the way in which they carry their old religious passion into their new anarchist beliefs, these form quite a category of their own in anarchism.

Jeronimo Caserio, the Italian who assassinated President Carnot of France in 1894, was twenty-one at the time and had been a fervent Catholic. A partial epileptic, he had dreamed of entering a seminary, of becoming a priest, even, as he said, an apostle. From the age of seventeen this fervour became channelled into anarchism, nourished by the poverty of the Lombard peasants which made him weep with anger. In no way did his personality change: he remained highly emotional, devoted to his mother and single-minded in pursuit of his ideas: he had no interest in women, sport, or leisure time activities. After his trial he wrote to his mother: 'You know how good my heart is, how gentle I was when I was close to you. Today my heart is still the same: if I have

Right: Emile Henry's bomb explodes in the Café Terminus. It was the random and unselective nature of many anarchist attacks which caused the particularly hysterical middle-class reaction

committed this act it is because I was tired of seeing the world so wicked.'

In Andalusia the same sort of 'religious' enthusiasm and moral indignation, fired the anarchist 'missionaries' who toured the villages converting the peasants to the anarchist faith.

'The few who held out [wrote the historian Diaz del Moral], whether because they were peaceable or timid or afraid of losing public respect, would be set on by groups of the *convinced* on the mountainside, as they ploughed the furrow, in the cottage, the tavern, in the streets and squares. They would be bombarded with reasons, with imprecations, with contempt, with irony, until they agreed. Resistance was impossible. Once the village was *converted,* the agitation spread . . . Everyone was an agitator. Thus the fire spread rapidly to all the *combustible* villages. In any case the propagandist's job was easy. He had only to read an article from *Land and Liberty* . . . for the hearers to feel themselves suddenly illuminated by the new faith.'

'The sun of righteousness'

In France the well-known anarchist writer Sebastian Faure had started adult life as a Jesuit novice: Emile Armand, the anarchist prophet of free love had been a militant of the Salvation Army: while the American anarchist Samuel Fielden had been a methodist local preacher and Sunday School teacher when living in Lancashire. Fielden's language showed how permanent was the imprint of his religious upbringing despite his revolt away from it:

'I trust the time will come when there will be a better understanding, more intelligence, and, above the mountains of iniquity, wrong, and corruption, I hope the sun of righteousness and truth and justice will come to bathe in its balmy light an emancipated world.'

The conclusion which begins to emerge is that anarchism had a number of social origins but that in many cases personal and intellectual reasons were predominant. On the intellectual side one finds that many anarchists had educated themselves and arrived at anarchism by reading or through discussion. In this sense they had more in common with the pioneers of socialism in the first half of the 19th century than with the unionised socialist workers of fifty years later. In 1897 a French social scientist, Dr Bailhache, carefully interviewed just such a self-taught anarchist. His name was Albert Lebrun and he was married with three children. Both he and his wife worked in a small Parisian factory producing cardboard. They had stable, if monotonous work, had experienced no unemployment for

twenty years, were adequately housed, and had a solid diet. 'I am purely a theoretical anarchist,' Lebrun said. 'I know that society as it exists is rotten but personally I have nothing to complain about.'

In 1880 after a period of socialism he had come across writings by Kropotkin and was deeply affected. By their sheer persuasiveness he was convinced that anarchism was right. Still more, the local anarchist group in La Villette had a library and Lebrun's wish was to read and educate himself. Within a few years he had opened a subscription library in his own quarter of Paris charging according to the means of the subscriber until a police raid caused it to close down. Thereafter, he continued to read and distribute anarchist pamphlets, though this was the extent of his action. Towards the terrorists he was understanding but could not share their belief in violence even though he held the bourgeoisie collectively responsible for the evils of society. All his ideas, concluded the interviewer, were from books, and even though his position continued to improve and he became the owner of a small piece of land in the country, he remained a convinced anarchist.

No generalisations can be drawn from this individual study though it is a good illustration of anarchism as an educating force. In particular, it helps to undermine the familiar stereotypes of the anarchist: the satanic conspirator, the bomb-throwing criminal, the social immoralist. All these may have a basis in fact, in the lives of certain anarchists, but when they are used as general definitions they tell us more about the people who use them than about the anarchists themselves.

Divided into several contrasting movements, socially of varied origin and showing a kaleidoscope of personal motivation, the anarchists defy a general explanation as they defy any aspect of authority. As we have seen, certain categories can be found and certain explanations offered but no generalisation can cater for the entrenched individualism of the anarchist tradition. Perhaps the most one can do in summary is to echo Malatesta's simple formula, 'Anarchism was born of a moral revolt against social injustice,' and then to turn to the drama and details of that revolt.

Left: The squalor and poverty of the slums — rag-pickers at work

Chapter II
Individual Terror

The action of anarchist revolt was known as 'propaganda by the deed'. There was never full agreement on the exact meaning of this phrase but the date of its acceptance as anarchist policy was crucial. On 1st March 1881 Alexander II, Tsar of Russia, was assassinated. Those responsible were not anarchists but a group of Russian revolutionaries called The People's Will, five of whom were hanged for the murder. At once leading anarchists expressed their full sympathy for the assassins, and when a congress of anarchists met in a public house in London on Bastille Day 14th July 1881, an agreement emerged that propaganda by the deed was to be encouraged, even though some like Kropotkin counselled moderation. Still further the congress decided to set up an Anarchist International, despite the failure of previous attempts, and to have regular annual meetings. Thus, the 'Black International' was born in the shadow of political assassination and, although it never met again, its existence and its acceptance of illegal action gave to late 19th-century Europe the myth of a well-organised anarchist conspiracy against all figures of authority.

The assassination and the congress made acts of violence the main talking point throughout the dispersed anarchist underworld, and destruction by individual action became the illegitimate heir to Bakunin's revolutionary urge. At first much of the violence was theoretical. Anarchist papers like *Le Drapeau Noir* (The Black Flag) in France explained how to make bombs and others encouraged anarchists to settle with authority 'in their own way'. By such means the anarchist readiness for destruction was made public and when a bomb was thrown into the café of the Bellecour Theatre in Lyons on 22nd October 1882 it was immediately presumed that anarchists were responsible and a young anarchist Cyvogt was convicted on flimsy evidence.

In the next five years Lyons anarchists were accused of three attempted fires and thirteen different bomb

Left: *The arrest of Emile Henry after he had thrown his bomb into the crowded Café Terminus at the Gare St Lazare in Paris*

attacks on targets which included a police station, two churches, a doctor's house, the law courts, and a monument to the Capucin monks. In Paris in 1886 a bottle of vitriol exploded on the floor of the stock exchange, thrown by a young anarchist Charles Gallo, who used his trial to preach anarchism for over an hour, while in Chicago in the same year occurred the notorious incident which gave the anarchists their first martyrs, but which established the black, destructive stereotype of the anarchist firmly in the American mind.

The first anarchist martyrs

On 4th May, a bomb was thrown into the Haymarket Square where thousands of Chicago workers were protesting against the shooting of strikers the day before. The police were in the process of breaking up the meeting and the bomb killed one of them instantly. The others opened fire on the crowd and several armed workers fired shots in return. In the general panic more policemen and a considerable number of workers were killed and Chicago reacted with hysterical anger. Seven anarchists were arrested and charged with the murder of the first policeman: another anarchist, Albert Parsons, gave himself up for trial, confident that he could not possibly be proved guilty on a complete lack of evidence. But the trial was a judicial farce: it was staged as the revenge of the forces of order against men who, in newspapers and speeches, had called for revolution and who were intimately involved in provoking the strikes and protests of the workers. There was no attempt to prove that they threw the bomb, it is still not known who did, but all were found guilty of murder by a jury whose admitted prejudices against anarchism were declared by Judge Gary to be 'no cause for their exclusion'. Four of the accused were hanged, Spies, Parsons, Engel, and Fischer; Fielden, Schwab, and Neebe were committed to long prison sentences, and the eighth, Lingg, who had fabricated bombs at various times, was found dead in prison after a bomb had exploded in his mouth. Fischer summed up the justice of the trial when he exclaimed: 'I was tried here in this room for murder and I was convicted of anarchy. I protest against being sentenced to death because I have not been found guilty of murder.' In 1893, the new Governor of Illinois re-examined the evidence and set the three prisoners unconditionally free. The jury, he said, had been packed, the jurors legally incompetent, the judge partial, and the evidence insufficient.

Right: A bomb is thrown at the police during a protest meeting in Chicago. This incident gave anarchism its first martyrs when four anarchists were executed after trial by a prejudiced jury

Les MARTYRS de CHICAGO

Exécution de PARSONS, SPIES, FISCHER, et ENGEL, coupables de propagande anarchiste

1. Parsons chantant dans sa cellule. 2. La marche au supplice. 3. Les martyrs, la tête enveloppée d'une cape blanche un moment avant la chute de la trappe.

The Haymarket Affair highlighted the fact that most of the Chicago anarchists, estimated at about 3,000, were of European origin with three of the regular anarchist newspapers written entirely in German. The spectre of international anarchism was thus added to the fear of revolution within the city and the anarchist-hunt which accompanied the trial accurately reflected the high level of public fear. The reconsideration of 1893 altered little, since by then the news from Europe was full of anarchist outrages. The era of Ravachol had begun.

By chance, neither of Ravachol's two Paris bombs in 1892 killed anybody, though they were aimed to destroy the magistrates who had convicted two anarchists for violent revolt in 1891. The significant point was that Ravachol had placed the bombs without knowing on which floor his intended victims lived, with the result that his violence was random, his destruction arbitrary. He might have killed the magistrates or he might have killed any of the other occupants. The only way to justify this was to claim that anarchism held the *whole* of the bourgeois world responsible for authority and that in principle there was little difference between the magistrate and anybody else who was wealthy enough to live in the big houses of the Boulevard St Germain. This was exactly Ravachol's answer. In prison he declared:

'The anarchist who blows up houses aims to exterminate all those who by their social status or their actions are harmful to anarchy. If he were allowed to attack these people openly without fear of the police and risk of his neck, he would not need to destroy their houses with dynamite, a method which can kill the household servants who are members of the downtrodden class.'

His opponents, therefore, were to be killed, not just removed from power, and the macabre quality of the songs inspired by his deeds made this intention widely known:

Dansons la Ravachole
Vive le son, vive le son
Dansons la Ravachole
Vive le son
De l'explosion!
Ah ça ira, ça ira, ça ira
Tous les bourgeois goût'ront d'la bombe
Ah ça ira, ça ira, ça ira
Tous les bourgeois on les saut'ra
On les saut'ra

(Let's dance the Ravachole, Long live the sound of explosion! Ah that will be fine. All the bourgeois will have a taste of the bomb. All the bourgeois will be blown up.)

Left: The Chicago 'martyrs' are led from their cells to be hung. Seven years later they were officially declared to be innocent

39

It was not that anarchists everywhere agreed with Ravachol. Influential leaders like Kropotkin and Malatesta roundly condemned his 'dangerous buffoonery' and made it clear that they, as anarchists, aimed at change, not at wanton destruction. But such statements disowning Ravachol received less publicity than the manifestos which supported him, and for the general public the only guide to anarchist principles lay in the events which the daily press chose to emphasise.

'Vengeance will be terrible'

In 1893-4 it could be argued that events chose themselves. From Spain, in November 1893, came the news that an anarchist had thrown two bombs into the Teatro Liceo in Barcelona where the audience in glittering evening dress were enjoying a performance of *William Tell*. Twenty people were killed and the anarchist Santiago Salvador claimed that it was an act of revenge for the execution of his friend Paulino Pallas who had thrown a bomb at General Martinez Campos, killing a soldier, five bystanders, and the General's horse but not the General himself. Pallas had exclaimed before being shot in the back, 'Vengeance will be terrible' and Salvador had exacted it. In return hundreds of anarchists were arrested, several were executed on charges for which there was no proof, and many were abominably tortured in the infamous prison of Montjuich, near Barcelona.

In France the spiral of destruction was repeated. In December 1893, Auguste Vaillant threw a home-made bomb filled with nails into the Chamber of Deputies, striking at the heart of the French political system. In the smoke and pandemonium several deputies claimed to be mortally wounded, but no one was, and Vaillant could not be found guilty of murder. He was executed, nonetheless, despite an effort by some of the deputies to secure his reprieve. A week after his execution the daily paper *Le Matin* carried the headline 'The Avengers of Vaillant, Bomb explodes in the Café Terminus'. Emile Henry aged eighteen, the son of an old Communard, had thrown his bomb into the crowded station café at the Gare St Lazare and had fled, firing on his pursuers before being overwhelmed by the crowd. He was a brilliant student, but coldly obsessed with the 'evil and wickedness of society'. 'I wanted to kill,' he said, 'and not just to wound like Vaillant. I hoped for fifteen dead and twenty wounded. Unfortunately only one person was killed.' His whole

Left: A bomb explodes in the Teatro Liceo in Barcelona during a performance of 'William Tell' in November 1893. Top left: Ravachol during his interrogation by the police. Bottom left: An allegorical print of Ravachol vanquishing the guillotine

manner was clinical and detached: he welcomed the sentence of death, refused to apply for a reprieve, and wrote poems and read Don Quixote before his execution on 21st May 1894.

A month later on 24th June President Carnot was assassinated at Lyons. An Italian anarchist, Santo Jeronimo Caserio, broke from the crowd which was applauding the President's carriage, handed him a piece of paper and under cover of the note stabbed him in the chest. The reason Caserio gave was that the President had refused to pardon Auguste Vaillant and was therefore technically guilty of murder. At his trial it was stated that he intended to return to Italy to kill the King and the Pope. 'Not both at once,' he replied, 'they never go out together,' a touch of wry humour recalled in 1900 when Gaetano Bresci, envoy of an anarchist group in Paterson, New Jersey, assassinated King Umberto of Italy in revenge for the repression of workers in May 1898.

Like King Umberto and President Carnot, the Spanish Prime Minister Cánovas del Castillo was also held responsible for judicial decisions made with his authority, in particular for the horrors of Montjuich which he had permitted. The role of avenger was assumed by another Italian anarchist Michele Angiolillo who left London, traced Cánovas into the Pyrenees, and shot him dead while he was sitting on a balcony with his wife, reading a newspaper.

By contrast, the assassination of President McKinley of America in 1901 was more an isolated event, and not part of a conscious pattern of oppression, assassination, and reprisal. But Leon Czolgocz, the assassin, was of Polish descent and it was known that he had attended an anarchist lecture by Emma Goldman, herself Russian by birth, so the certainty increased throughout America that anarchist terror was international, an imported disease whose carriers should be compelled to return to their own countries before further contamination took place. Legislation soon followed to prevent the entry of anarchists into America, and after the First World War those of foreign origin who remained were deported.

In the Russia which Emma Goldman had left anarchist terror was more co-ordinated than in France, Spain, Italy, or America, though it emerged at a later date: it was not until 1903 that anarchist groups became a sizeable part of the gathering revolutionary momentum. In the revolution of 1905, provoked by the gunfire of the Tsarist guards against a workers' demonstration, two anarchist groupings, *Chernoe Znamia* (Black Banner) and *Beznachalie*

Right: Troops execute six anarchists in Barcelona in 1894. Savage persecution prepared the way for a more serious revolt

(Without Authority), centred at Bialystok and St Petersburg, established themselves as the leading exponents of systematic and random destruction. Gangs, armed with pistols and home-made bombs, profited from the breakdown of Tsarist control by murdering local officials, landlords, and industrial employers. The mood was also one of self-destruction; several anarchists were killed by their own bombs or blew out their brains in order to avoid arrest, while in Odessa a bomb laboratory was run by a Polish anarchist and his wife who entertained their friends by dancing the cake-walk, bombs in hand.

The failure of the 1905 Revolution removed the cataclysmic drive of the Russian anarchists, though their violence continued in the face of severe repression. Elsewhere in Europe the graph of anarchist terror had curved downwards after 1900, though France produced a crop of marginal anarchists who specialised in armed robbery and murder. The most famous was the elusive Bonnot gang which filled the crime pages between 1911 and 1913. Bonnot himself became a legendary figure, a bandit of the Al Capone vintage, who died pressed between a mattress, riddled with the bullets of the police whom he had defied in the most sensational gunfight of his own violent career. His relentless sequence of crimes brought comparison with the era of Ravachol, but by 1911 individual terror had lost its appeal and few anarchists rallied to the defence of Bonnot as they had done for the acts of Ravachol. The 'heroic' decade had been the 1890s, the *fin de siècle,* translated optimistically by certain anarchists to mean 'end of the bourgeois society'.

But society survived, not without moments of considerable fear and the price the anarchists paid for the terror was a reputation for being satanic and subhuman.

Clearly, anarchist destruction of the bomb-throwing, murderous variety, was seen with horror as an attack on property, established interests, and authority. But beyond this there were other reasons for the virtual dehumanisation of the anarchist in the public mind. In the first place there was, as we have seen, the widespread belief that the dagger, dynamite, and pistol were the tools of an organised international threat to humanity. This was a useful explanation for those who ignored the misery and injustice in their own society and who refused to see that anarchism could spring spontaneously from their own slums and social ghettos, but it cannot be dismissed solely as a fabrication. Historians know that the various events of violence had no coherent plan and that the Black International existed only on paper, but the public at the time

Left: The end of a violent career—Bonnot dies pressed between a mattress after his sensational gun fight with the police

had no means of knowing, and the governments always suspected an international plot, even when they found little evidence of it. Even if no more than a coincidence, the simultaneous appearance of anarchist violence throughout Europe and America gave it an international flavour and the wave of assassinations led obviously to the question, who and where next? The violence was thus seen to involve not just the political stability of one regime or another but the order and stability of all countries. It was easy to argue from this that the anarchists believed in total and universal destruction.

Secondly, as observed by Thomas Hobbes in the 17th century, man's worst fear is not just death, but violent and unexpected death. Anarchist violence, with its strong element of random terror, provoked this extreme fear in those who were imminently threatened. Human beings have erected elaborate rituals and rules for killing each other, by wars, slavery, persecution, and execution, but the anarchists appeared to ignore them. Their violence was therefore labelled as 'insane' and 'inhuman'. By comparison, the mass execution of thousands of Communards in 1871 or the organised slaughter of millions of soldiers in the First World War were seen as strictly according to the rules, however much to be regretted.

Thirdly, anarchist violence was accused of being a revolt against man's basic nature. Authority, it was generally believed, is natural to man: the father was held to be a natural authority to his son, and the men of superior talents to those who were less gifted. The anarchists, by denying the inevitability of authority, were thus denounced as rebels against nature, and their destructiveness as an absurd and desperate attempt to defeat the natural process. Lombroso even suggested that anarchist assassination was a kind of indirect suicide. Assassins like Henry and Caserio, he said, despaired of the world but lacked the courage to take their own lives. They therefore murdered, knowing they would be executed, a complete repudiation of life, abnormal and unnatural.

How did the anarchists meet these reactions? How did they justify their violence in the face of public horror and hostility? When Emile Henry was condemned to death *The Anarchist,* an English paper, concluded its editorial:

'Men like Emile Henry may be in error, but they are at least sincere. There is no greater proof of a man's sincerity than that he will lay down his life for a cause. And Ravachol, Pallas, Vaillant, and Henry have done this.

We say to the rich, if these men are monsters you have created them. You who have butchered the people whole-

sale for your greed. Can you be surprised if from their blood should arise the avengers?

Is it right to kill, to kill the innocent to attain riches and power? Then it is right to kill those who are responsible for the murder of the innocent. And who are responsible? All those who live idly upon the robbery and the murder of the workers . . .

Our modern civilisation is a Moloch temple reared upon the bodies of slaughtered slaves. Let the terrorists do what they will, they cannot equal the crimes of our masters.'

The full ingredients of the more moderate anarchist position are contained in this extract. Extreme publications like the French *Manifesto dedicated to the memory of comrade Ravachol, assassinated at Montbrison by executioners paid by the bourgeois of the French Republic* went further, and revelled in the prospect of bloodshed, concluding: 'The bourgeois have sown the wind, they shall reap the tempest.' But the justification is the same: anarchist terror is presented as self-defence, justice, and revenge.

'Your hands are covered in blood'

The personal justifications of the terrorists were almost all in the same vein. They offered their own violence as a mirror to the violence of society. 'Your hands are covered in blood,' said the judge to Emile Henry. 'Like your red robes,' replied the anarchist. As individuals they fundamentally endorsed the famous phrase of Bakunin, 'the urge to destroy is also a creative urge', and saw their destruction in a positive way, as an act of demolition so that better things might be built. Life was to come out of the flames and ashes of death, an image which recurs in theories of resurrection and rebirth throughout Western culture. The hold of this image over the imagination of anarchists gave them confidence and a martyr-like dedication. Ravachol's bombs may have been disclaimed by many anarchists but his vision of the future was a common one. Out of anarchist action he saw the emergence of a golden age:

'No more wars, no more quarrels, no more jealousy, no more theft, no more assassination, no more police, no more judges, no more administration.'

Vaillant, even more than Ravachol, paraded the justice of his act. He had first come to Paris at the age of thirteen travelling without a ticket. Caught by the railway officials, he was brought before the magistrates who in-

Right: In Russia anarchism often went hand-in-hand with the other movements seeking the overthrow of Tsarism. The house of the prime minister Stolypin in 1906 after one of the unsuccessful attempts to kill him. He was finally assassinated in 1911

formed his parents. But neither his mother nor his father wanted him back and for the rest of his adolescence he was alone, living in acute poverty and imprisoned twice for minor offences. He began to educate himself and, in contact with anarchist circles developed a passion for libertarian ideas as well as natural history, astronomy, and philosophy. He emigrated to South America but returned in 1893, as poor and unsuccessful as ever.

'Everywhere I have been,' he stated in court, 'I have seen unfortunate creatures bent under the yoke of capitalism. Everywhere I have been, I have seen the same wounds and tears of blood. Tired of this life of suffering I aimed my bomb at those who were primarily responsible for social misery. The explosion of my bomb is not just the cry of a rebellious Vaillant but the cry of a whole class which demands its rights.'

This speech concludes, as well as any, the anarchist case for violent propaganda, terror, and destruction. Vaillant had meant to injure and was pleased to state that 'a hundred deputies lay wounded on the floor'. He had not meant to kill, whereas other anarchists made death in quantity their aim. But his words are typical of the many anarchists who designated themselves as martyrs to a cause beyond themselves.

In point of fact most of the terrorists were isolated individuals, but they rarely saw themselves in this way. 'There are thousands to continue the work', exclaimed Pallas. 'Mine is not the last head you will cut off', said Henry, while in the Ukraine, Matrena Prisiazhniuk, convicted with two others for terrorism, declared:

'Proudly and bravely we shall mount the scaffold, casting a look of defiance at you. Our death like a hot flame will ignite many hearts. We are dying as victors. Forward then! Our death is our triumph.'

Anarchist terror cannot be understood unless it is set within this conviction: it was seen as part of a growing human revolt which history would justify. By such reasoning, violence was proclaimed as the midwife of change.

Right: Vaillant's bomb explodes in the Chamber of Deputies. After the dust and chaos had died down, it was found that no-one had been killed. Nevertheless Vaillant was guillotined

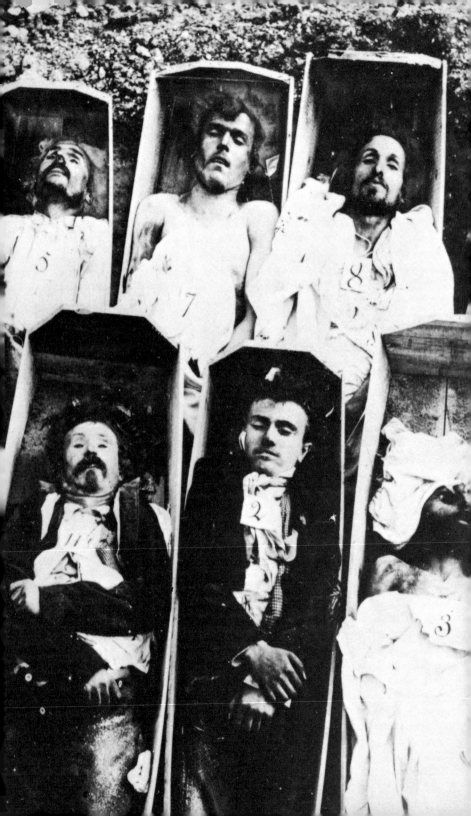

Chapter III
Collective Revolt

In March 1907, a tolerant reviewer in the *Times Literary Supplement* wrote:

'The anarchists of the newspaper and novel who occasionally murder a sovereign or a president but more often kill a number of innocent bystanders, are either weak-minded fanatics or common criminals who have picked up a theory spun by more ingenious brains than their own and use it as a justification of their criminal acts. The real anarchists never do anything of the kind, or, indeed, anything at all except talk and write . . .'

By 'real' anarchists he was referring to Kropotkin, whose famous treatise, *The Conquest of Bread,* he was in the process of reviewing. Certainly, by comparison with the individual terrorists, Kropotkin and the other leading theorists of the time looked academic and inactive, withdrawn into the fastness of political science.

But this is to underestimate the active role of their propaganda which provoked and inspired the rank and file of the anarchist militants. Their 'propaganda by the word' was aimed at inciting anarchist action: their mere 'talking and writing' was a campaign to wake the slumbering discontent of the exploited classes into revolt. This was the legitimate tradition deriving from Bakunin; revolutionary teaching to bring revolutionary action, the 'creative action of the masses'.

Kropotkin, it is true, lends himself easily to the reviewer's interpretation. Not only did he condemn Ravachol and preach moderation in violence but he lived for over thirty years from 1886 to 1917 in peaceable exile in England, occupying small houses in Brighton and Hammersmith where he played the piano, wrote his many books, pamphlets, and letters, and gave tea to a wide variety of intellectuals. 'He was amicable to the point of saintliness,' said George Bernard Shaw. 'His only weakness was the habit of prophesying war within the next

Left: The bodies of Communards after the rising in Paris in 1871 had been crushed. Although not controlled by anarchists, the rising went into anarchist folk-lore as the model for a popular revolution against all aspects of established authority

fortnight.' But this 'weakness' is the significant point. Kropotkin's vision of revolution infected anarchists throughout Europe and his pamphlets, which denounced authority as evil, circulated from one group to another, spreading intellectual certainty that anarchy was not only right but the creed of the imminent future. In Geneva in 1903 a few of his Russian disciples issued a paper called *Khleb i Volia* (Bread and Liberty) named after Kropotkin's book and incorporating several of his articles. They adopted as the slogan of the paper Bakunin's phrase 'the urge to destroy is also a creative urge' and it was this paper which was smuggled into Russia and fed the revolutionary enthusiasm of the newly formed anarchists at Bialystok. In such ways Kropotkin's 'writing and talking' became potent agitation, a result totally approved by this 'amiable saint'.

Similarly in France, appeals to the masses flowed from the pens of Elisée Reclus, like Kropotkin an eminent geographer, Jean Grave, the 'Pope' of the anarchist Rue Mouffetard, and Sebastian Faure the Jesuit novice turned vehement anticlerical. Their writings through newspapers alone reached at least 10,000 readers and during the Ravachol era they were accused of instigating revolt, even when they disowned the bombs and random terror. After Vaillant's bomb the Chamber of Deputies was presented with a bill to curb anarchist journalism by making any support for violence a criminal offence. By this method the highbrow writings of Jean Grave in *La Révolte* as well as the scurrilous slang of Emile Pouget in *Le Père Peinard* became the object of police prosecution and the two newspapers were forced to close down in 1894. Sebastian Faure provides a good example of the propagandist at work in the speeches he wrote for anarchists who were brought for trial. As a powerful orator, his voice can be heard in this defence of Léveillé, who was tried in August 1891 with two other anarchists for an armed demonstration:

'Let me briefly sketch a picture of modern society. At the top there are priests engaged in the traffic of sacraments and religious ceremonies, soldiers selling secrets of a so-called national defence, writers glorifying injustice, poets idealising ugliness, shop-keepers giving false measure, industrialists faking their products and speculators fishing for millions in the insatiable sea of human stupidity. At the bottom there are building labourers without homes, working tailors without clothes, working bakers without bread, millions of workers beaten down by unemployment and hunger, families heaped up in slums

Right: 'The right to steal' — a cartoon distributed during the Commune pillories capitalists and all other exploiters of the workers

54

LE DROIT
AU
VOL
par
Nadar

SYSTEME
DU
PLUS LOURD
que L'AIR

...lot E. Picard... Marchand de journaux
...et achète toutes les valeurs.
...gagné avec ARTHUR
...quelques misérables millions en tripotant
à la
BOURSE

and young girls aged fifteen forced to earn money by enduring the sweaty embrace of old men or the rapacious assaults of the young bourgeois.'

The only result of this gross inequality and injustice, the speech ended, will be the revolt of increasing numbers until 'universal Revolution ushers in the anarchist ideals'.

'The model of anarchist revolution'

Sebastian Faure's conviction was shared by most of the leading theorists, despite the range of disagreement among them. The anarchists in Chicago who were hanged for the crime they did not commit, Errico Malatesta who was hounded by the Italian police, yet spent years of relative calm in England, Emma Goldman who was incensed with anger after the Chicago hangings, all these, like Kropotkin and the French intellectuals were knowingly responsible for inflammatory propaganda. They encouraged revolt and supported it when it came.

In the 1870s, hopes of revolt lay either with the Jura watchmakers or with the personal dynamism of Bakunin, but it was Paris, defeated by the Prussian army, which provided a model of what an anarchist revolution might be. The Workers' Commune, declared in March 1871 as a revolt against the French Government, was neither planned nor controlled by anarchists, though individual anarchists were among its most passionate supporters. But it was an example of a single locality taking the direction of its affairs into its own hands and, as such, measured up to one of the cardinal prescriptions of anarchism, local autonomy. Among the Communards, Proudhon was a more acknowledged master than Marx, and his solution of federalism was to some extent envisaged, since an independent commune was also proclaimed at Lyons, and lesser attempts made in other French towns.

Two further factors entrenched the Commune in anarchist memory. Firstly, in the Paris streets working-class men and women had organised their own society with a high degree of moral idealism. Even though several priests, including the Archbishop of Paris, were killed and in the final days many official buildings of Paris were set on fire, the wall posters and legislation of the workers' government show that destruction was not their aim. Even the Bank of France was left intact despite the poverty and famine which undermined the Commune

Top right: *A posed photograph of Communards being shot by government forces. The savage reprisals were never forgotten.*
Bottom right: *Another example of the Republic's willingness to use force against its underprivileged to keep them in their place—troops fire in a May Day parade at Fourmies in 1891*

from its very beginning. Secondly, when the troops of the French Republican Government moved in to end the revolt, the Communards were killed in their thousands, shot like animals in mass executions. No anarchist forgot this savage repression. When Emile Henry threw his bomb into the Café Terminus in 1894, an English anarchist paper reminded its readers of Henry's parentage: 'Henry is the son of a man who has seen thousands of working men, women and children shot down in heaps, while well-dressed men and dainty ladies struck the bound prisoners with canes and parasols shrieking "Shoot them all!"' This was the legacy of the Commune, an image of bourgeois brutality which remained more vivid than the optimism stirred by the first achievements of working-class Paris.

It was not until January 1892 that a collective revolt reawoke the dreams of an autonomous anarchist society. With shouts of 'Long live Anarchy!' 4,000 Spanish peasant labourers marched into the town of Jerez waving sticks, scythes, and other agricultural implements. Their driving force was hunger, the intense hunger which gripped the Andalusian villages in the winter, but their slogans were anarchist: 'We cannot wait another day, we must be the first to begin the Revolution. Long live Anarchy!' For several hours they held the town, but they could offer no serious resistance to the police who later made sure that the repression was severe. The anarchist peasants had done little except look for food, in the course of which two shopkeepers were killed, but four of the 'rioters' were executed and about twenty sentenced to long periods of hard labour.

The Jerez march drew attention to the fervour of the Andalusian anarchists, to their passionate admiration for Bakunin, to their hopes of a millenium when all land would be held in common, and to their periodic strikes, broken as they were by landowners calling in blackleg labour from the mountains. But the march itself was more a restaging of the old peasant revolts than an anarchist revolution and the most the European anarchists could say was that it pointed heroically to the future.

In the years that followed, propaganda by the deed was sidetracked, in Spain as elsewhere, into individual terrorism, an expression of the desperation in most anarchist circles. The era of revolution in which Bakunin had flourished was now no more than the nostalgic property of old men. Eminent anarchists like Kropotkin, Malatesta, and Faure, continued to express revolutionary

Left: *Police break up a strike meeting in Germany. Despite the resistance of the authorities in every country, the use of strikes as a weapon of the increasingly better-organised working class spread rapidly in the early years of the 20th century*

hopes and to redefine the ideas of spontaneous revolt, but many of the young recruits to anarchism saw the machinery of a popular rising as clumsy and ineffective, superseded by new methods. For results they looked either to the quick, incisive action of the assassin or, increasingly, to the new phenomenon of anarcho-syndicalism.

The growth of *syndicats,* French for trade unions, had brought into common parlance the concept of syndicalism. By 1900 this concept, originally meaning trade union activity for higher wages and better conditions, had come to assume revolutionary overtones. The change was within the trade union movement itself, where the exponents of syndicalist theory developed the idea of the general strike as the great climax to revolutionary economic action. The pioneers of the theory were French trade unionists, many of whom were anarchists at the same time, and from their combination of anarchist theories and trade union activity developed the phenomenon of anarcho-syndicalism. It was a militant movement pointing to the trade union as the vital source of mass action, at once more powerful and more creative than either individual terrorism or spontaneous revolt.

The need for self-education

In France, one outstanding personality became inseparable from this major development in collective anarchist action: Fernand Pelloutier. Only thirty-four at his death Pelloutier gave a structure and purpose to revolutionary syndicalism which reflected his own deep concern for educational and constructive values. The revolution, he believed, must be constructive, but he had little faith in the untutored creativity of the masses. He, on the contrary, argued that the working classes were the victims of bad education or none at all and that the governments had deliberately kept them in submissive ignorance. Education must therefore be undertaken within the trade unions themselves, by the workers for the workers, and his overriding preoccupation was to initiate and activate this process of self-education.

In 1895, he was elected general secretary to the *Fédération des Bourses du Travail* (labour exchanges) which, at the time, were independent of the trade union movement. In this position he set himself to transform his modest organisation into a model for working-class education, in which the ideas of anarcho-syndicalism were to be taught as the answer to a century of frustrated revolutionary hopes and illusions. Working first alone, then

Left: *A meeting of anarchist-led workers in Barcelona shortly before the strike which began the rising against the authorities*

with his assistant Paul Delesalle, Pelloutier established three areas of action: firstly, a service of mutual aid by which, he declared, the *Bourses du Travail* would become a state within a state controlling every service relating to working-class improvement; secondly, an educational service, with the ambition of making the *Bourses* and the *Syndicats* into the working man's university; and thirdly, a propaganda service to extend the ideals and practice of anarchism and to provoke collective organisation of production and consumption.

Racked with pain from tuberculosis, Pelloutier spent the last years of his life dedicated to extending his projects among anarchists who were suspicious of all organisation and among syndicalists who were slow to see the importance of education. By his death, in 1901, he was revered as the master spokesman of anarcho-syndicalism, a clear sign of his success with both groups. A year later his *Bourses du Travail* were united with the *syndicats* and in 1906 the combined force of French syndicalism known as the CGT *(Confédération Générale du Travail)* produced its revolutionary manifesto in the Charter of Amiens, which cut all ties with political parties and asserted the supremacy of economic action. If Bakunin was the distant master of anarchist revolution, Proudhon was the ancestor of anarcho-syndicalism, and Pelloutier his most imaginative descendant.

The enthusiasm generated by the revolutionary syndicalists in France spread into other countries and by 1907, when a congress of anarchists met in Amsterdam, the relationship of anarchists to trade unions was the main point of contention. Should anarcho-syndicalism and its trust in the general strike be allowed to replace the Bakuninist tradition of revolution by spontaneous uprising? How, in other words, should the 'creative masses' assert their freedom? Pierre Monatte, aged twenty-five, closely influenced by Pelloutier, spoke first:

'One must be blind,' he stated, 'not to see what anarchism and syndicalism have in common. Both aim at the complete destruction of capitalism and the wage system by means of social revolution. Syndicalism is the reawakening of the labour movement: it has recalled anarchism to its working class origins.'

He then stressed the methods of syndicalist action, strikes, and sabotage, the latter to be used whenever strikes were unable to break the resistance of employers.

'The spirit of revolution in France,' he added, 'was dying year by year. Then syndicalism was born, the spirit

Left: *Nuns flee from their convent during the rising in Barcelona. The workers equated the Church with political oppression and this led to widespread destruction of religious buildings*

was revived, and for the first time since anarchist dynamite silenced their proud voice, the bourgeois trembled.'

In reply Errico Malatesta spoke for his generation's confidence in popular revolt. Syndicalism he portrayed as inevitably conservative, working within the established economic system for legal ends. It could not, he argued, be revolutionary since trade unionists were not even agreed among themselves but defended their sectional economic interests against each other. Anarchists should join trade unions, he said, but for propaganda purposes, and to prepare for the collective control of production when the revolution arrived. As to the revolution itself, the general strike might be useful at the initial stages but it could not replace the armed insurrection of the people. Only a popular revolt could ensure an anarchist future, and he concluded:

'The anarchist revolution which we want transcends the interests of a single class: it envisages the liberation of all humanity which is at present enslaved, either economically, politically, or morally. We must guard ourselves from any action which is unilateral. Syndicalism, excellent as it is for activating the working class, can never be the unique anarchist method.'

Other speakers put the case against Monatte even more vehemently, condemning even the fight for an eight-hour day as a diversion from true anarchist principles, but the Congress did not arrest the expansion of syndicalism, nor the recruitment of young anarchist workers into trade union activity. To Monatte and those he represented, the older anarchists seemed no more than strident voices from the past, with nothing to contribute to the present.

Then in July 1909, to the delight of both sides, occurred the Barcelona rising. 'What is happening here is amazing,' wrote the anarchist Anselmo Lorenzo to a friend. 'A social revolution has broken out in Barcelona and it has been started by the people. No one has instigated it. No one has led it. Neither Liberals, nor Catalan Nationals, nor Republicans, nor Socialists, nor Anarchists.' This was not the government's version. In a telegram to King Alfonso XIII, the Prime Minister, Antonio Maura, talked of a 'seditious movement' and throughout the crisis the government believed that a conspiracy was responsible. In fact the week of rioting, later known as the *Semana Trágica* (Tragic Week) was as near to a spontaneous revolution as the followers of Bakunin could have hoped. Lorenzo was right: the masses took to violence in an unplanned defiance of central authority.

Far left: Barcelona in flames during the rising (top). Graves opened by the workers (bottom). Left: Government troops who were sent swiftly in to re-establish control over the whole city

Barcelona was in no way a surprise setting for revolution. Both the city and its region, Catalonia, had a long history of mistrust and hostility to the government in Madrid and, as the main industrial centre of Spain, it was the focus of a growing working-class consciousness. Peasants had come from the countryside to take jobs on the docks or in the textile factories, and brought with them the teachings of rural anarchists. Urban anarchists were growing in strength among the badly paid workers, and Marxist socialism was equally represented. In periods of calm it was a rival to anarchism but at times of crisis and opportunity mutual action was possible. Finally, the mob orator Alejandro Lerroux, neither socialist nor anarchist but a vehement republican, was the most vigorous single revolutionary force in the city and his years of fiery rhetoric had kept the workers alive to the possibilities of revolt. But none of these forces planned the rising. If anything the government was responsible, for, after a military setback in Morocco, they called up the reservists in Catalonia, most of whom were working-class family men, strongly antimilitarist ever since they or their fathers had returned starving, and ridden with malaria, from the colonial war with the United States in 1898. Memories of the disastrous campaigns in which Spain had lost Cuba, the Philippines, and Puerto Rico were bitter, and the workers saw the government's move as a deliberate act of class warfare and exploitation from the centre. In addition they saw the black hand of the Church behind it, since it was widely rumoured that the Morocco campaign was to protect iron mines owned by the Jesuits.

The rising of the people

On Monday 26th July, the workers replied to the call-up by a general strike, declared by an anarchist and socialist committee. Already troop trains were being delayed by women sitting on the rails, and with the strike the labour force of Barcelona poured into the streets to protest against further departures of trains or men. In the city, trams were overturned and communications cut. By Tuesday Barcelona was in the hands of the people, though no direction and organisation were visible, not even from the strike committee. Barricades were thrown together against the army and police who by Thursday had mounted a substantial counterattack, and behind the barricades there was looting of food shops and wide-scale destruction of religious buildings.

Left: The execution of Ferrer. As a leading free-thinker he was held morally responsible for the Barcelona rising. 'Aim well, my friends, you are not responsible. I am innocent'

The Catholic church in Spain had made its social decision in the 19th century by its alliance with the wealthy, the employers, and the forces of government and order. By the 20th century, most industrial workers identified the Church with political authority and moral exploitation: anticlericalism had thus become integral to working class politics. The burning of convents and other desecration which characterised the Barcelona rising was an acting out of this emotional fury against an oppressive institution. It was even more than this: it was a bold defiance of religious taboos. Workers danced in ecclesiastical vestments, coffins were opened, and the corpses of nuns scattered on the pavements. Ostensibly this was mere destruction but the desecrators were clearly testing the power of the Church, exposing the mystery and occult forces of Catholicism as powerless in the face of irreligious attack.

But if the rioters had shown that no divine power would intervene to defend the Barcelona convents, they were not so successful with the temporal power. By the end of the week the government had regained control and although the rioters had generally respected the lives of nuns, monks, and priests, their desecration of property and their offence against religious sensibilities was not to be forgiven. Over 150 working men and women were killed in the streets as the rebellion collapsed, and summary executions followed the restoration of order. Unable to find any obvious conspirators the government arrested the leading Spanish anticlerical and educational reformer, Francisco Ferrer, who had been in London during the events and had no part in the rising. Ferrer, to the outrage of traditional Catholicism, had started the *Escuela Moderna* (Modern School) in Barcelona where children were to be educated in a free-thinking, nonreligious way. His manner was pedantic and his passion was for educational theory, but he was in touch with anarchist circles and the printing press used for his adult classes produced a stream of anarchist literature. To the Catholic hierarchy his schools were 'in league with the devil', 'worse than brothels', and equated with anarchism of the most destructive type, and they held him morally, if not actually, responsible for the Barcelona revolt. On these grounds he was condemned and shot. To the execution squad he cried, 'Aim well, my friends, you are not

Right: A parade in Paris to protest against the savage reprisals which followed the crushing of the Barcelona revolt. *Far right:* A cartoon shows priests looking at their new 'cross' — the handles of the garrot which was used to execute so many of the rebels *(bottom)*. Training the heir of the King of Spain to be a good son of the church like his father — he plays with the head of Jules Ferrer who was executed after the rising *(top)*

responsible. I am innocent. *Viva l'Escuela Moderna.*'
Within days there were demonstrations throughout
Europe against this political murder, and the protests
were not just from anarchists but from all sections of
liberal society. The pressure was in part successful for
King Alfonso dismissed the Prime Minister Antonio
Maura who had argued for Ferrer's death as a deterrent
against further revolution.

But had there been a revolution at all? By comparison
with the Russian Revolution of 1905 the Barcelona rising
was no more than a few days of dramatic news. The
'creative masses' of the anarchist dream had barely had
time to realise their opportunity and nothing of a constructive nature was achieved. But the fact that the
people could rise without the planning of a professional
revolutionary body was seized by those who had supported Malatesta at the Amsterdam congress as a justification of their revolutionary theory.

But what had surprised the Barcelona workers themselves was the immediate success of the general strike
which they held to have been the catalyst for the revolt.
The anarcho-syndicalists made maximum propaganda
from this fact and the anarchist trade unions emerged as
the main beneficiaries of the rising. In October 1910, a
year after Ferrer's execution, a conference uniting
anarchist and other libertarian unions from all over
Spain formed the *Confederacion Nacional del Trabajo*
(CNT) which at once became the most dedicated syndicalist movement in Europe. In its organisation it respected the anarchist emphasis on autonomy: the unions
were to be local ones and not vast national concerns and
all the administrators were to be unpaid and imper-
manent. Subscriptions were to be extremely low and
there were to be no strike funds. By such methods the
CNT sought to incorporate the principles of spontaneity
and voluntarism within a loose structure, and thus reach
a viable compromise between freedom and control. In
one sense it succeeded, for, whatever its record, the CNT
expressed the basic attitudes of Spanish anarchism: a
strong moral purpose, intense hostility to the Church,
local autonomy, and a millenarian hope of a golden
anarchist future.

From 1910 to the Spanish Civil War in 1936, the CNT
remained anarchist in leadership and inspiration. It did
not substantially improve the condition of the Spanish
workers, nor did it produce a social revolution despite
numerous general strikes which paralysed industry **75** ▷

Left: *A French left-wing poster of strikers confronting troops.*
Next page: *The middle-class nightmare—a cartoon shows the*
squalor which would ensue if the lower classes gained power

in various localities at different times. But it nurtured a passionate sense of liberty for which its members were willing to kill and be killed, and when the Civil War broke out it stepped naturally into the vanguard of the republican defence, sparing no violence in its moral crusade against the forces of Franco and Spanish nationalism. In November 1936, the man who had come to symbolise both the CNT and Spanish anarchism, Buenaventura Durruti, was killed, and in the public tributes paid to this worker and military leader the full flavour of Spanish anarcho-syndicalism emerges. To a crowd outside the war ministry in Madrid, Frederica Montseny spoke of the grief of Durruti's comrades:

'We all feel that we have lost something very precious to us, something like part of our own body. All Spain must feel the same, because when a man acquires the category of a symbol, this man is no longer a representative of a tendency, he is no longer just a comrade and a friend. He becomes a representative of the whole people. And now that we are creating a new Spain and from this Spain a new world, where a new society is being created by rivers of blood, Durruti will be the symbol of all of us, with his undying faith in himself and in the triumph of justice and the ideal which we pursue . . .'

And at the end of her speech she called for collective vengeance:

'Durruti my brother, my friend, inseparable companion to all those who have fought by your side, we still dream with you, laugh with you, and together with you defy death. Durruti my brother, my friend, all of us who lived with you, loved with you, fought with you, and suffer with you, swear by the innocent head of your little daughter. We swear to give our last drop of blood to revenge you.'

This was collective revolt as it emerged in Spanish anarcho-syndicalism. Ideas forged in France and defended for several years by French anarchists had become the property of Spain, and in this new setting they gained a revolutionary vigour which the French CGT had been unable to sustain. For Spain the debate staged at the Amsterdam congress in 1907 had been decisively resolved. Despite the spontaneity of the Barcelona rising in 1909, despite the almost mythical fame of Bakunin in rural Andalusia, the bulk of the Spanish anarchists opted for the syndicalist method of collective action. In so doing they pushed anarchism for the first time into the forefront of a nation's politics.

Although the CNT became the major exponent of anarcho-syndicalism in Europe, its achievements were

Left: *A painting by Pelizza da Volpedo of Italian workers on strike*

75

dramatically eclipsed at one point by events in Italy. Italian anarchism had been a history of strenuous propaganda by individuals like Carlo Cafiero, Saverio Merlino, and Errico Malatesta who published papers, started numerous small groups, and spent their lives outwitting the vigilant Italian police. The orthodoxy was Bakuninist, with a rich outcrop of variations, though in the eyes of the outside world Italian anarchists were the leading apostles of individual terror, the cloak and dagger anarchists, both real, like Caserio, and imaginary. What encouraged this reputation, besides the actual assassinations, was the fact that many Italian anarchists lived for long periods in exile and were believed to be international conspirators. As a result Italy was thought to be a forcing house of anarchist theory and practice, whereas in reality anarchism inside Italy was fragmented and generally weak, though influential in certain towns like Carrara, Ancona, and Leghorn.

It was to Ancona that Malatesta returned in 1913, after thirteen years in London, to launch a revivalist campaign among the disintegrating anarchist groups of the area. He returned in the spirit of his Amsterdam speech to counter the growing appeal of Italian syndicalists who had formed their own organisation on the French model in November 1912. Known as the *Unione Sindicale Italiana* it was a revolutionary break-away from the larger socialist trade union movement, the CGL, and was recruiting steadily among anarchist workers, particularly railwaymen and building labourers. Malatesta had no wish to sabotage this new collective action but rather to strengthen the resolve of other anarchists, in the belief that Italy was on the verge of a revolutionary opportunity. This was almost entirely a piece of intuition, but between 1913 and 1914 he raised the expectancy of anarchists by a tireless sequence of meetings, speeches, and conversations under the guise of a Circle of Social Studies.

Then in June 1914 the Ancona police fired on a group of demonstrators, killing three workers and wounding several others. Immediately the town broke into revolt and the police retreated to their barracks. Malatesta himself told the rest of the story.

'The government tried to prevent the events of Ancona from being telegraphed to other parts of the country: but nevertheless by and by the news became known and strikes broke out in all the towns of Italy. The two Federal Labour organisations, the General Confederation of Labour, which is reformists, and the *Unione Sindicale,* with revolutionary tendencies, proclaimed a general strike, and were joined by the Railwaymen's Union.

Right: The spirit of revolution leads the workers during Red Week

These strikes and demonstrations in several towns provoked new conflicts with police, and new massacres. At once without any common understanding, one place ignorant of what the other was doing, as communications were broken off, the movement assumed everywhere an insurrectional character, and in many places the Republic, which meant for the people the autonomous Commune, was proclaimed.

'All was going splendidly; the movement was developing and the railway strike, spreading on all lines, paralysed the government: the workers were beginning to take measures of practical communism with a view to reorganising social life on a new basis, when suddenly the Confederation of Labour, by an act which has been qualified as treachery, ordered the strike off, thereby throwing the workers into confusion and discouraging them.

'The government was not slow to profit by the condition, and began to restore "order".'

As in Barcelona the strikes and revolts lasted for a week, Red Week as it became known. It seemed at one point as if the regime was seriously imperilled but the monarchy survived, Malatesta returned to England, and Italian anarchists reoccupied their twilight world waiting for the new dawn. Not even Malatesta could hide the significant role which the unions had played. The transient success of Red Week had been commensurate with the success of the general strike: nothing could blur this very real justification of anarcho-syndicalism. On the eve of international war it had established itself as the most potent method of collective anarchist action.

But as a theory of revolution was it based on just as many illusions as the theories of Bakunin, Kropotkin, and Malatesta? Did it suffer like so much of anarchism from over-optimism? The Marxist socialists certainly thought so. Throughout this period anarchists were opposed not only by the forces of order but also by the socialist parties who saw anarchism as purely utopian. Anarchists were dismissed from the First International and, although they attended the early congresses, excluded from the Second International after 1896 by a socialist majority. Although they became a driving force in syndicalism it was only in Spain that they became dominant. Marxists proved stronger in the American attempt at a national labour organisation, the Industrial Workers of the World (IWW): they outpaced the anarchists in the French CGT, and in England the moderate reformist elements kept both anarchists and doctrinal Marxists at bay. In most countries the ideological conflict was mainly a propaganda one, a rivalry of recruitment, newspapers, and ideas, but in Russia the tension between Marxism and anarchism finally broke into violence.

'Anarchic windbags'

The Russian Marxists were well prepared for a struggle with anarchism. At the end of the century Georgii Plekhanov, one of the most respected pioneers of Russian socialism, wrote a scathing attack on anarchist ideas, called *Anarchism and Socialism,* in which he reduced writers like Kropotkin and Jean Grave to the level of children playing games with words. The foreword to the English edition sets the tone: 'There are those who think that the precious time of so remarkable a writer and profound a thinker as George Plekhanov is simply wasted by pricking anarchist windbags. But unfortunately there are many of the younger, or of the more ignorant sort who are inclined to take words for deeds, mere sound and fury for revolutionary activity, and who are too young and too ignorant to know that such sound and fury signify nothing.' Plekhanov himself was just as scornful:

'A wit [he writes] has said that the profession of faith of the anarchists reduces itself to two articles of a fantastic law. (1) There shall be nothing. (2) No one is charged with carrying out the above article.

This is not correct. The anarchists say: (1) There shall be everything. (2) No one is held responsible for seeing that there is anything at all.

This is a very seductive "ideal" but its realisation is unfortunately very improbable.'

In their turn the *Khleb i Volia* group of anarchists attacked Plekhanov and Lenin in 1908 as the 'priests, magi, and shamans' of the modern age and denounced the Marxist concept of the dictatorship of the proletariat as a tyrannical notion, as evil as any bourgeois authority. In the revolution of 1905, which failed to overthrow the Tsar, this fundamental gulf was widened by the anarchists' random use of terror, and in the following years the anarchists were themselves divided, as elsewhere, by the issue of anarcho-syndicalism. When the February Revolution of 1917 erupted they were in no sense a united group capable of transforming the discredited Tsarist Russia into a new society. But the Bolsheviks were, and when Lenin's October Revolution was successful the Marxist claim to be scientific where the anarchists were utopian appeared to be justified. A hard, practical pursuit of power had triumphed.

It was not that the anarchists had undermined the Revolution. On the contrary they had been one of the forces to oppose and disrupt the liberal provisional government from its beginning, but they remained implacable enemies of government in any form and the

Left: *The scene in Milan as workers gather for a demonstration*

arrival of Lenin to power followed by the assertive rule of the Bolshevik party, cast them once again into the role of opposition. Many of them talked of a third Revolution between 'Social Democratic power and the creative spirit of the masses' and during the winter of 1917-18 bands of Black Guards were formed, though several anarchist leaders spoke out against a revival of random terror. The Bolsheviks were far from satisfied with this verbal moderation and decided on repression. In April 1918 they acted. Raids were carried out by the secret police on twenty-six centres of anarchist Guards within Moscow itself. In some there was no resistance but in others heavy fighting broke out leading to the death of forty anarchists and the arrest of 500. The Bolshevik police lost twelve of their agents. From the Petrograd anarchists came an immediate denunciation: 'You are Cains. You have killed your brothers. You are Judases, betrayers. Lenin has built his October throne on our bones,' and in the provinces a contagious outbreak of anarchist terror spread through towns and villages as a defiant protest against the new authority.

Not all anarchists were implicated. Two months after the Moscow arrests the popular peasant anarchist Nestor Makhno arrived in the capital and had a tactical talk with Lenin on the defence of the Revolution. Makhno, although impressed by the Bolshevik leader, rejected his taunt that the anarchists were dreamers, and returned to his native village in the Ukraine to organise his own peasant army. The village was occupied by Austrian troops under the terms of the Treaty of Brest-Litovsk, by which huge areas of western Russia had been ceded to the German-Austrian forces, and Makhno found that his mother's house had been burned to the ground and his brother shot dead. With an anger which infected all who met him, he set in motion a guerilla warfare of revenge, striking daringly at the heart of the Austrian occupation. His band of anarchist partisans came together for lightning attacks then merged back into the agricultural labour force exchanging guns for farm implements, while the peasants too old to fight serviced him with food and transport.

Deeply respected for his human qualities, Makhno showed himself to be a military leader of exceptional stature. Although he fought under the black flag of anarchism his major attribute was brilliant organisation and control of his men, and in this he anticipated the achievements of Durruti and other CNT leaders in

Left: *Bolshevik soldiers during the October revolution. There was a long tradition of hostility between anarchists and the Bolsheviks before 1917, and in April 1918 a Bolshevik attempt to eliminate anarchist supporters led to wide-spread revolts*

the Spanish Civil War. When his own campaign became part of the Russian Civil War his legendary victories against the Austrian troops assured him a place alongside the Red Army. But they could not work together for long and as Makhno continued to insist on the independence of his army the Bolshevik press inserted references to him as an 'anarcho-bandit'.

'Liberty or Death'

Throughout 1919 the uneasy alliance held, mainly due to Makhno's surprise victory against the White Russian army of Denikin at Peregonovka in September. Shortly after, he liberated the town of Ekaterinoslav and the slogans of his army 'Liberty or Death' were translated into social terms. The citizens were given liberty to live and work as they wished, and freedom of speech and organisation was proclaimed, with a proviso dissolving all Bolshevik groups. But applying an independent peasant mentality to urban affairs was unsuccessful and many industrial workers were unable to make themselves, their co-workers, or their factories function on the anarchist principle. Makhno's ideals of freedom were not, therefore, universally welcomed as a charter of deliverance, and the Bolsheviks labelled the experiments as a return of bourgeois individualism.

In the winter of 1919 Trotsky ordered the Red Army to dislodge Makhno's partisans from their hold over the Ukraine, but the incursion of another White Russian army forced the rival Bolsheviks and anarchists together for a final campaign. Promises were even made by the Bolsheviks to liberate all imprisoned anarchists but once the campaign was successfully over these were forgotten. In November 1920 Makhno's headquarters were decisively raided and many of his colleagues and staff summarily shot. He himself escaped, and in 1921, known ironically to some in the West as a ruthless Bolshevik leader, he arrived in Paris. He died in 1935, and was buried unceremoniously far from the Ukraine in a Parisian grave.

In the last period of fighting Makhno had not always recruited his men by kindness alone and stories of his terrorist persuasion were picked up and used to propaganda effect by the Bolshevik regime. It is doubtful whether the conflict was a simple one between anarchist liberty and Bolshevik authority and the cause of Makhno's guerillas was not helped by the incidence of anarchist destruction elsewhere. But the conflict was not protracted, for by 1922 Russian anarchism had been liquidated, after a brief period of hope in March 1921 when, fifty years after the Paris Commune, the town of Kronstadt rebelled against Bolshevik authority. The

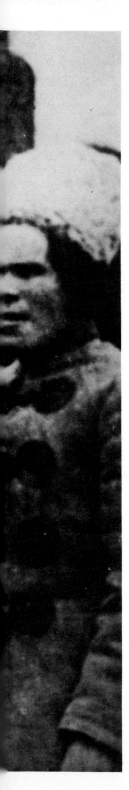

suppression of this rebellion was tantamount to the final destruction of libertarian opposition, and anarchism became one of the many 'counter-revolutionary' practices outlawed from the new Russia.

In part this was, as Victor Serge pointed out, the fault of anarchist obstinacy and blind idealism. Serge had been a militant anarchist in France before the war, but rallied to Lenin's Revolution as the best that could happen in the real world. He advised other anarchists to do the same.

'It is a fact,' he stated in 1921, 'that the Revolution could not have been successful without organisation, centralisation, and the creation of the Red Army. If anarchists repudiate these lessons they condemn themselves to the past and to failure: they will be guilty of turning their back on reality, history, and opportunity.'

Those who remained anarchists could not see the issue in this way. Throughout the anarchist world the Russian Revolution was described as a great moment in history, tragically betrayed by authoritarian Bolshevism. Emma Goldman, deported from the United States in 1919, had arrived in Russia, the country of her birth, early in the next year. Like Kropotkin, who had returned in 1917, she had high hopes that the Revolution would be the climax of the native revolutionary tradition, the tradition of Bakunin. In February 1921, Kropotkin, the 'gentle anarchist', died, his disillusionment known to his close friends and shared by many of the anarchists among the 20,000 mourners who followed his coffin through the frozen streets of Moscow. In December of the same year Emma Goldman left the country in despair:

'It was just one year and eleven months [she wrote] since I had set foot on what I believed to be the promised land. My heart was heavy with the tragedy of Russia. One thought stood out in bold relief: I must raise my voice against the crimes committed in the name of the Revolution. I would be heard regardless of friend and foe.'

For the first time in the West the anarchists had a sympathetic audience. Even the terrors of anarchy paled before the reality of Red Revolution, and the anarchist victims of the Bolshevik regime have been seen as minor symbols of liberty by the capitalist opponents of Soviet Russia. It makes an ironic epitaph for those who had staged so many acts of collective revolt against authority and capitalism.

Left: Makhno, the Russian 'anarcho-bandit' leader with his staff

Chapter IV
Freedom and Anarchy

In 1960 *Freedom,* the English anarchist weekly, carried out a survey of its readers by means of a questionnaire. The majority of the 358 who replied in Britain described themselves as individualist or philosophic anarchists: over 80 per cent declared they had no religion; over 90 per cent belonged to no political party; over 70 per cent had received some form of further education or training after leaving school, and the most popular papers read were the left-wing 'heavies', *The Guardian, The Observer,* and the *New Statesman.*

Of course it can be argued that only people with higher education, philosophic interests, and highbrow reading habits answer questionnaires and therefore these figures prove nothing about the modern British anarchist. But even so the results establish the presence of a sizeable body of serious-minded, free-thinking individualists within the orbit of British anarchism. No doubt the relative strength of this kind of anarchist has increased over the years but at the turn of the century the tradition of free-thinking individualism was already well established. Alongside the bombs, strikes, and street revolutions there were anarchists intently pursuing individual freedom. For some this meant a public campaign, since freedom for one implies freedom for all; for others it meant social withdrawal, a rejection of the norms of society. But in theory, if not in practice, there was wide agreement: the freedom they demanded was freedom from ignorance, superstition, and moral prejudice.

Freedom *from* is a negative position. In positive terms the demands were for new methods of education, a secular approach to man and society, and liberty to make one's own moral decisions. When anarchy was frequently attacked as a 'golden society in which goods and sex are free' this was a hostile but not inaccurate picture of what many anarchists considered to be ideal.

Anarchist education is invariably associated with

Left: Children at school at the turn of the century. Anarchist educationalists tried to break away from rigid teaching methods and to allow children to develop their true desire to learn

85

Francisco Ferrer, owing to his martyrdom at the hands of Spanish religious and political authority. He was in fact well known in libertarian circles before his death, and his modern school in Barcelona was the object of imitation in other countries. Ferrer was the son of peasants who were zealous Catholics, but in his first job he came under the influence of his employer who was a persuasive atheist, and fifteen years in Paris between 1886 and 1901 saw the hardening of a lifelong hostility against the Church. He was there as an exile after participation in an abortive Republican revolt, and he became interested in the French public educational system, admiring its freedom from religion though criticising its subservience to political authority.

Outside the state system there was one institution which had a particular impact on Ferrer, the orphanage at Cembuis near Paris, directed from 1880-94 by the anarchist Paul Robin. The aim of Robin was to show that a child was not condemned by the poverty or ignorance of his parents to a life of inevitable squalor and misery. Sympathetic education and outdoor life was the challenge he threw down against the ill effects of heredity and early environment. In the words of Emma Goldman, 'he took his material wherever he could find it. From the street, the hovels, the orphan and foundling asylums, the reformatories, from all those grey and hideous places where a benevolent society hides its victims in order to pacify its guilty conscience. He gathered all the dirty, filthy, shivering waifs his place would hold and brought them to Cembuis.' Here the power of a pleasant environment and Robin's skill as an educator were pitted against the child's underprivileged background, and his success gave rise, in 1897, to a 'League of Libertarian Education' which tried to raise funds for its own school. A limited amount of money was found, not enough for a school, but enough for two anarchists to take nineteen boys and girls to a house in the country for a month's education, but much of the idealism was dissipated when one of the anarchist supervisors began hitting the children. In a tactical retreat the League turned to adult education.

By close observation of Robin's institution, and sharing the initial enthusiasm of the ill-fated League, Ferrer reached his own theory of education. When he returned to Spain, in 1901, the school he had in mind was one to

Far right: Two leading anarchist educationalists — Francisco Ferrer who founded the Escuela Moderna *(Modern School) in Spain (top) and Sebastian Faure (bottom) who began its French equivalent 'The Beehive'. Right: Slum children play in the streets. Ferrer and Faure set out to prove that their background need not always condemn these children to a life of squalor and boredom*

liberate the child from all restricting authority whether political, religious, or moral. The education he offered in his Modern School, to the scandal of the Spanish Church, was called 'Rational Education' and it owed much to the spirit of the European Enlightenment, the ideas of Rousseau, and the Positivist tradition which enshrined science as the only means to knowledge. 'Rational education,' wrote Ferrer, 'has, in the first place, no regard to religious education, because science has shown that the story of creation is a myth and the gods legendary . . . On the other hand, our teaching has nothing to do with politics. It is our work to form individuals in the full possession of their faculties, while politics would subject their faculties to other men.'

What then was the basis of the modern school? 'All the value of education,' Ferrer stressed, 'rests in respect for the physical, intellectual, and moral will of the child . . . the real educator is he who can best protect the child against his [the teacher's] own ideas, his peculiar whims; he who can best appeal to the child's own energies.' The emphasis was thus on learning and expression rather than on teaching, on freedom for the child to develop according to his abilities rather than on timetables, syllabus, and discipline. This in itself was revolutionary in the context of rigid Spanish education, though the logic of such freedom was that a child with religious interests should be allowed to explore and develop them. But Ferrer stopped short of such logic: his militant atheism meant that freedom was the antithesis to religion – the child should be spontaneous, self-expressive, and free but within a non-religious structure.

Such was the power of Ferrer's anticlericalism that he converted a rich orthodox Catholic lady to his ideas and when she died she left her money to him, enabling him to set up the Modern School on a firm financial basis. It was not, therefore, an impoverished experiment like much of anarchist education elsewhere, though money did not ensure it against Church and State interference. In 1906, Ferrer was imprisoned on a charge of complicity in a bomb attack on King Alfonso and the Queen. The bomb had been thrown by a librarian from the Modern School, and although Ferrer was found not guilty, the school was forcibly closed. His execution three years later ensured that it never reopened.

Ferrer had taken many ideas from France but in turn his own theories were reflected in French anarchism where Sebastian Faure was the leading child educator.

Left: *Troops in action during the 'Sidney Street siege' in London. Three suspected anarchists barricaded themselves in a house and soldiers eventually had to be employed to kill them*

In 1904 he had founded *La Ruche* (The Beehive) and within three years it had become the French equivalent of Ferrer's *Escuela Moderna*. Situated in the country, 'The Beehive' was a boarding school for orphans and poor children whom Faure wished to deliver from the evils of both Church and State schools. Classification of the children in order of merit was abolished and the staff, drawn from anarchist colleagues, were unpaid, taking what they needed to live from a common fund. 'The Beehive,' Faure declared, 'is the school of the future, dedicated exclusively to the child.' The education given was closely geared to social teaching: in arithmetic the children were given sums to demonstrate how wages could be made more equal, and in history Faure stated 'we explain to our children that true history is yet to be written —the story of those who have died, unknown, in the effort to aid humanity to greater achievement.'

The quest for adult education

The Beehive lasted until the First World War cut its financial resources, which were almost entirely Sebastian Faure's earnings as a lecturer and writer, and in 1917 this single-minded experiment came to an end after three last struggling years. Internationally it was less celebrated than Ferrer's Modern School, partly because Faure was one of several innovators in the French educational world, whereas Ferrer stood out sharply in the Spanish scene. In fact Ferrer was not entirely isolated since the Andalusian anarchists had attempted to form their own school, but the educational effort of most anarchists in Spain tended towards adult education. Ferrer himself actively promoted evening classes, and in the province of Malaga a women's educational society enrolled 20,000 members from rural occupations, whereas in Barcelona the anarchists had a foot in the Polytechnic Academy where the director, Tarrida del Marmol, was an anarchist militant.

In other countries the same generalisation holds: despite the lead of Robin, Ferrer, and Faure in child education, it was adult education, the instruction of the parental generation, which was given priority. This was more in keeping with anarchist philosophy: adults came for education voluntarily and whenever they wished; children, even the forty children of the Modern School, needed occasional coercion and, despite the Beehive's example, schools tended to become institutions with a paid staff and bureaucracy.

Left: *Police are issued with arms and ammunition during the Sidney Street siege. This was the nearest that England came to the anarchist violence which terrified the rest of Europe*

91

In the adult sphere Fernand Pelloutier was the master anarchist mind and leading innovator, and his Bourses du Travail, as we have seen, were envisaged as a kind of popular university. As a boy he had been expelled from a religious school for writing an anticlerical novel, had then shown signs of brilliance at his secondary school, but had failed his exams. He left to become a journalist, and part of his commitment to education derived from his experience of propaganda through the written word. The workers, he decided, were over-submissive to bad conditions and poor wages because they rarely read anything to enlighten them. For this reason he started a workers' periodical, *L'Ouvrier des Deux Mondes* (Worker of Two Worlds), which became one of the pillars of his educational system, and stood as a class rival to the long-established academic periodical *Revue des Deux Mondes*. The rest of his programme hinged on an imaginative series of lectures and discussions and, in general, on the propaganda education of being an active anarcho-syndicalist and participating in economic action. In the widest sense Pelloutier's aim was to make the worker intelligently aware of his condition and the prospects of changing it. In his own words, the trade union should be 'a practical school of anarchism'.

The workers' friend

In the same year that Pelloutier took over the *Bourses du Travail*, 1895, a German bookbinder, Rudolf Rocker, arrived in the East End of London. His boyhood had been spent in a Catholic Orphans' home in the Rhineland city of Mainz after the early death of his parents, though his uncle showed a paternal interest and instructed him in social problems, encouraging the boy's capacity for serious study. Due to this influence Rocker became a socialist at a time when Bismarck's anti-socialist legislation restricted agitation. This legislation, he recalled, 'developed in me a profound aversion for the brutal suppression of ideas and personal convictions'. From socialism he turned to anarchist writings and as a result of his activities he was forced to leave Germany in 1893 and seek refuge first in Paris, then in London.

It was the East End that attracted him and revealed his strong missionary drive, which, like Pelloutier's, was to enlighten the submissive and lead the militants into action. His first contact was with a Jewish anarchist circle in Whitechapel and, although he himself was not a Jew, he dedicated his time to learning Yiddish and after three years became the editor of the Yiddish paper *Der Arbeter Fraint* (The Workers' Friend) which he ran until 1914. Using the paper as a point of departure, rather than as an end in itself, Rocker moved outwards

into workers' education. His concern was mainly for the depressed and exploited Jewish tailors in the sweatshops of East London, whose successful strike in 1912 was largely due to his enthusiasm and organisation. In 1906 the Jubilee Street Institute was opened and workers were invited to participate in lectures and classes of the most varied nature, from histories of the working class to studies of Russian poetry. Immigrants from Eastern Europe were given English lessons and helped to assimilate into English life, though there were many provocative references in the newspapers of the time to the 'foreign anarchists in our midst'. These remarks grew to a torrent of protest when, in December 1910, a gang of desperadoes, at once denounced as anarchists, shot three English policemen during a raid on a jeweller's shop in Houndsditch, and finally barricaded themselves in a house in Sidney St in Stepney. Troops were deployed by Winston Churchill, the Home Secretary, and the men were killed after a dramatic siege which was the nearest England came to the era of Ravachol. But the anarchist connection of the robbers was a conclusion based on coincidence. One of them had been wounded by the police at the time of the robbery and was traced to the house of a girl who made no secret of her attendance at anarchist meetings. Furthermore, a card with Malatesta's name was found in her house alongside material used for breaking and entering left by the wounded robber. Assumption was taken for proof and the siege of Sidney St was backed by a barrage of newspaper articles on conspiracy and black revolution. The girl, however, turned out to know virtually nothing about the robbers, and Malatesta had been involved merely by giving the robber, who told him he was a mechanic, an introduction to places which stocked mechanical equipment.

Rocker was not implicated in person, but the publicity threatened his activities, which had to undergo the close scrutiny of the police. His innocence of all subversion did, however, emerge and his educational achievements among the most deprived workers of the East End were recognised by a wider public. This is not to say that his anarchist ideas became safe or popular, or that he was fully accepted into English society. When war broke out he was interned as an enemy alien and in 1918 he preferred to return to Germany. But his name he left behind in Whitechapel where he had so powerfully entered the history of Jewish labour. 'May God bless you,' an old Jew had said to him. 'You have helped my children in their need. You are not a Jew, but you are a man!'

Left: *Tolstoy with his sister-in-law — 'I regard all governments as institutions for committing the most revolting crimes'*

Most of these anarchist pioneers in education condemned the orthodox schools and colleges as reactionary, and harmful to the child or student. Some went even further and appeared to condemn education itself as unnatural and coercive. Paradoxically the major spokesman for this position was the great literary figure of 19th-century Russia, Leo Tolstoy. The author of *War and Peace* did not style himself as an anarchist, because he held the word to imply violence and destruction, but many of his followers used the term and, during his long life, he was often referred to by others as a passive or Christian anarchist.

Strongly moved by the horrors of the Crimean War and the scene of a public execution in Paris in 1857, Tolstoy became a lifelong opponent of authority which he held directly responsible for the evils he had witnessed. 'I regard all governments,' he emphatically stated, '. . . as intricate institutions sanctified by tradition and custom, for the purpose of committing by force and with impunity the most revolting crimes.' In his treatise *What then must we do?* (1886) he also attacked the towns as a degenerate influence on the lives of ordinary people. He described in remarkable detail the miserable quarters of Moscow and went on to hold the rich, the State, and the Church responsible, arguing that in a Christ-like society there would be no Church and no State. What then was to be done? Everything that comes from authority should be rejected: men should renounce money and territorial possession; industry as the cause of poverty should be suppressed; the towns as the cause of corruption should be vacated; education as the cause of arrogance should be restricted and, finally, men should return to the sanity of rural life.

Although he ran a popular publishing business, producing cheap editions of good literature, Tolstoy, the aristocrat, made many personal gestures in support of his simple, rural solution. At his country home he made his numerous children work in the fields with the peasants, and he frequently lectured the peasants on the evils of urban life. Because he had given up smoking at one stage he encouraged the peasants to do the same and even dug a ditch for them to throw their tobacco in. As to education he believed that wisdom lay in the rural commune, in its simple life, and in the natural goodness of the peasant. This was a view held in the mid-19th century by the Russian Populists and in the 1870s thousands of them left the towns and went to the country to discover peasant life and drink in the wisdom of the soil. Their idealism was rudely shattered when they encoun- **99** ▷

Left: *Tolstoy breakfasts with his family at Yasnaya Polyana. It was here that he set up his school for the local peasant children*

Anarchism in the Arts

While the Anarchists were attacking lack of freedom in politics and society at the beginning of the 20th century, many artists were beginning to break away from established taste and use their skills to attack social injustice. Impressionist and post-Impressionist painters like Pissarro and Signac (see pages 101 and 103) were breaking new ground in technique, and subsequent movements such as Surrealism (*below:* a scene from *Le Chien Andalou* made by Dali) and Dadaism (**below right:** the poster for an early exhibition) seemed to go to completely anarchic lengths to shatter bourgeois hypocricy and established ideas. Stimulated by the works of playrights such as Hauptmann and Wedekind, other writers continued to develop the essentially anarchist belief that art and literature should serve a social purpose. **Above right:** A poster for Jarry's controversial play *Ubu Roi*. **Right:** A costume for Genet's *Les Paravents* in which he bitterly attacked French involvement in Algeria

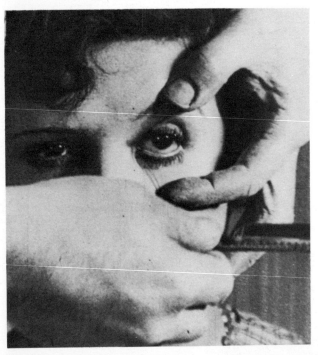

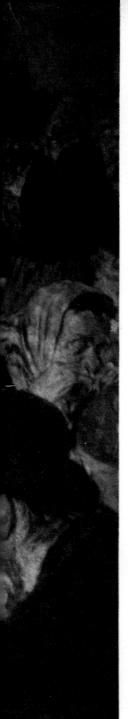

tered the boredom, discomfort, and ignorance of village existence. Many of the peasants were so suspicious of their unsolicited disciples that they treated them as police spies sent by the Tsarist government.

Tolstoy, however, never lost his faith in primitive goodness, and in his description of the local village school, *The School at Yasnaya Polyana,* he showed what he meant by the peasant child's natural intelligence and good sense:

'The teacher comes into the room where on the floor lie screaming children shouting "You are choking me" or "Stop it! Don't pull my hair" and so forth.

'"Peter Mikhaylovich," a voice at the bottom of the heap calls out to the teacher as he enters, "tell them to stop!"

'"Good morning, Peter Mikhaylovich!" shout the others continuing their game. The teacher takes the books and gives them to those who have gone with him to the bookcase; those who are lying on top of the heap, without getting up, also ask for books. The heap becomes smaller by degrees. The moment the majority have books, the rest run to the bookcase and cry "Me too, me too! Give me yesterday's book!" and so forth. If there are two left who, excited from the struggle, keep rolling on the floor, those who have the books cry out to them: "Don't bother us! We can't hear a word! Stop now!"

'The excited boys submit and, out of breath, take hold of their books and only at first, while sitting at their books, keep swinging their legs from unallayed excitement. The fighting spirit takes flight and the reading spirit reigns in the room!'

Learning, therefore, says Tolstoy, is as natural as fighting, and not to be forced, and he goes on to condemn exams and all attempts to grade and classify children as irrelevant to this natural process of learning. Tolstoy, therefore, is not hostile to a village education which gives 'full liberty to the pupils to study and settle their disputes as they know best': he reserves his scorn for the education of the towns which, he claimed, forces the child away from his spontaneous inclinations and gives him ideas remote from the reality of everyday life. To this extent he is not so far from the other anarchist educators as at first appears.

Where he really separates from people like Ferrer and Faure is in his Christianity. Tolstoy looked back to the early Christians, to their simple unquestioning faith, to their pacifism, and to their absence of organisation, and said: *'There* is the faith which moved mountains.' The Church, he stated, with its inner politics, its stress on

Left: The life of the urban poor — an Italian painting of a cheap dining room which typifies the need which many artists at the end of the century came to feel to use their skill to portray social evils

authority, and its links with the State had obliterated this simple Christianity and lost all touch with the teachings of Christ. To Gandhi, his great disciple, he wrote a letter in 1910 exposing the hideous contradiction in the Christian West between the law of love and the violence practised by the government, the army, the law, and the administration. He exhorted his brothers in Asia to live lives of passive resistance and not to resist evil by evil. Perhaps, he added, they would succeed where the Christians had failed.

'Who created God?'

Very few anarchists agreed with Tolstoy on the original virtues of Christianity. They shared his anger against the Church but went further and rejected religious faith altogether. They attacked the idea of God as a monstrous fraud, mounted by centuries of authoritarian priests, and they argued that the rituals and sacraments of any religion were merely a way of extorting money and obedience from the ignorant poor. Man could only be truly free, they proclaimed, if the hold of religion over his mind was broken. Freedom from superstition was thus a demand almost identical to freedom from ignorance, though the anarchist campaign for a secular view of man and society was not a distinctive one. They shared common ground with many atheists and anticlericals who were far from being anarchists. In particular they showed the same kind of sardonic scorn used by many opponents of religion. Paraf-Javal, one of the French individualists, dealt with religion in one sentence: 'If God created the world, who created God?' and left it at that, while another French anarchist, Emile Digeon, wrote in his last will and testament:

'I deny the useless existence of a god, creator and sovereign authority of the universe, invented by the priests of all religions in order to exploit the credulity of their followers. I especially reject the God of Christians or Catholics whose so-called ministers have made him, in their own image, a monster of pride and cruelty. Having played hide and seek with men throughout their miserable life, this god presents himself to them at their death and submits them to the most atrocious tortures if they haven't honoured him enough, or if they have given way to instincts and desires which he gave them in the first place.'

A multitude of similar statements can be found both in and outside anarchist writings. The problem for the anarchist was how to strike at religious authority with more power and effectiveness than the written word. In

Right: 'Kew Gardens' by Pissarro the Impressionist painter whose anarchist ideas led him into exile after the Paris commune

Spain desecration of religious buildings was one of the answers, as seen in the Barcelona rising of 1909, while in France theft of church property was a favoured method, particularly among the individual terrorists. Marius Jacob, leader of a French gang that preceded Bonnot, stated proudly in court in 1905:

'I have burgled lots of priests' houses. In all of them I have found a safe, sometimes several — and they didn't contain dried fish, believe you me, but large sums of money which imbeciles had given to God and which the priests were "looking after". And these are the charlatans who dare to call me a thief. But I'm a nice person and I don't hold it against them. I give them my blessing. Amen.'

But neither desecration nor theft was the main anarchist method of asserting freedom from religion. In anarchist eyes the Church was not just hypocritical, it was also the guardian of private morality and therefore an intolerable restraint on individual liberty. The assertion of *moral* freedom was thus the positive way chosen by many anarchists to show their opposition to religion. The aim was both to shock religious sensibilities and, more creatively, to release the repressed and censored emotions of the individual in a direction which they saw as healthy for himself and for society.

In the summer of 1905 a speaker arrived to give a public lecture in Montmartre, Paris, dressed only in a pair of bathing pants. His subject was nudity. He had emerged from his house, without any other clothes, onto a crowded street and was immediately arrested by two policemen who took him to be questioned. To the police sergeant he introduced himself as a medical student and explained his lack of clothing. Heat, he said, produced perspiration and perspiration contained harmful products such as uric acid. If perspiration therefore remained on the inside of clothes it would be reabsorbed by the skin and would poison the body. The sergeant heard him out with mock patience, concluded he was mad, and called for the police doctor. But the doctor, after listening to the student, said that from the scientific point of view he was quite correct, and since he had hidden his sexual organs under his pants there was no reason why he should be prevented from giving his lecture.

This account was given by a French anarchist by way of introduction to Ernest Lucien Juin known as Emile Armand, the anarchist prophet of sexual freedom. Armand was not the speaker but he was in the audience and thoroughly approved of the student's behaviour. It was faithful, he said, to the spirit of anarchist indivi-

Left: *'Harbour at Portrieux' by Paul Signac another anarchist artist who struggled against 'Bourgeois and official conventions'*

dualism which maintained that ideas should always be put into practice. If one was against clothes one should on no account wear them.

Armand both as man and writer fascinated his contemporaries. His early life was the opposite of most anarchists. Although his father fought in the Paris Commune and gave his son an intensely anticlerical upbringing, Armand became passionately religious. In London during his family's exile he bought a New Testament for a penny and thought the words of Christ had a freshness which his father's ideas totally lacked, and, when back in France, he began to go to meetings of the *Armée du Salut* (Salvation Army). In 1889, listening to a sermon on the text, 'You must be born again', he made a public act of religious commitment, and remained a soldier of Christ for the next eight years. But two factors began to make him restless and uneasy. In 1895 he was introduced to anarchist writings and at the same time he grew increasingly estranged from his wife. They had entirely different attitudes and quarrelled frequently. After one spectacular quarrel in 1897 the Salvation Army reduced him in rank, a punishment which he bitterly resented.

In reaction he tried to leave both the Salvation Army and his wife, but could not bring himself to break with his ingrained moral principles. But the break came in an unexpected way. Asked by the Salvation Army to deliver two hundred francs to a printer he became obsessed with the desire to steal it, and finally did so. That night he felt 'a great joy at having released himself from morality', and although he was plagued with guilt and eventually paid back the money, he had found out what he meant by freedom, the exercise of his own individuality. Immediately he turned to journalism and pamphlet writing to spread the light of individualism as he conceived it, and as a consummation of his freedom he separated finally from his wife in 1902. The reason he gave for breaking his marriage is the key to all Armand's writings: the sexual act, he said, between people who do not care for each other is immoral and unfree.

The use of the word immoral here was not a light piece of cynicism: Armand rejected orthodox morality, in fact all morality which came from outside the individual, but he taught in its place a new morality which he held to be more spontaneous and closer to the great human values of love and respect. Thus the reason for leaving his wife became the reason for making a 'union' with a woman he loved, Marie Kugel, since in his positive terms, the sexual act between people who cared for each other was both moral and free. The bulk of his work, therefore, was a carefully phrased argument that sexual freedom should be based on one individual's respect for another. This was

the message he preached with the zeal instilled by years of outdoor evangelising with the Salvation Army. His seriousness was not always recognised and he was often stigmatised as an immoralist, and for these critics he reserved his most shocking epigrams: 'There is today no essential difference between bourgeois marriage and prostitution' or 'Marriage is long-term prostitution; prostitution is short-term marriage'.

The right to sexual relations

In essence Armand claimed for the individual the full right to sexual relations with anyone who reciprocated his or her feelings, but his clinical, and often sentimental, language makes sure that this freedom is not taken in either a promiscuous or licentious sense. This can be seen when he distinguishes between the sexual desire and the desire to have children:

'When love is first born between two individuals and they unite with each other, they are not motivated by the desire to have children, but by sympathy and passion for each other, an attraction which finds its natural expression in the sexual act. The desire of the united pair to have children is an entirely different thing: in general it develops later and as a result of reflection. In consequence it cannot be seen either as a basic need or an instinct.'

From this distinction he derives the moral necessity of contraception:

'The man who respects the personality of the woman who gives herself to him would be negligent and authoritarian if he did not tell her that there are mechanical methods for preventing unwanted maternity.'

Armand lived until 1962 by which time his views were less controversial, but in 1901 when he started his first newspaper *L'Ere Nouvelle* (New Era) there were few precedents for his thorough-going individualist morality. But the outrage he provoked was of small dimensions compared with the storm which met Emma Goldman's campaign for birth control in the United States.

Emma Goldman had emigrated from the Jewish ghettos of Tsarist Russia at the age of sixteen in 1885. By 1889 she was a militant member of anarchist circles in New York, impelled by a burning indignation against the social injustices she had found in the 'land of opportunity and freedom'. The Chicago hangings had horrified her and the powerful writings of a German immigrant anarchist, Johann Most, had convinced her that anarchy was a positive solution. Under his influence she envisaged the possibility of violence and supported an assassination

Left: Gerhardt Hauptmann whose plays earned Emma Goldman's approval for the strength of their social commitment

105

attempt on the life of a leading industrialist in 1892. But by the 1900s she had drawn closer to the ideas of her other mentor, Peter Kropotkin, and had developed her own style of anarchist propaganda. Lecture tours quickly established her as a leading anarchist authority on individualism and the rights of women, and her journal *Mother Earth* founded in 1906 and named in a moment of spring optimism, explored the intellectual range of anarchism including its creative and literary aspect. She was implicated in the assassination of President McKinley in 1901 by the mere fact that the assassin Leon Czolgocz had attended one of her lectures, and although legally cleared of all suspicion the slur remained and in certain families the black, dreaded name of Emma Goldman was used to frighten the children.

In 1915 she moved boldly into an open discussion of contraception, not to be seen as her major preoccupation, but yet another of the many causes adopted by this restless reformer in her fight against established morality and what she saw as harmful prejudice. She herself was unable to have children due to an inverted womb but she had responded to the alarming facts of unwanted pregnancy which faced her in her tours of working-class America, and she saw in the lack of birth control a system which enslaved the individual woman. In *Mother Earth* she had advanced arguments for freedom in sexual relations, and since 1900 she had been giving private advice on methods of contraception. Her stand in 1915 was thus the public expression of a conviction which she had held for most of her anarchist career.

In 1916 she was arrested in New York after one of her lectures on 'the medical question', and her trial gave her an excellent platform for a rhetorical expansion of her subject, to the delight of artists, intellectuals, and sympathisers who came to the court to hear her. Condemned to a fine or fifteen days in prison she chose the latter, and her imprisonment did even more to rally radical support for her principles. 'In 1916,' wrote Margaret Anderson, 'Emma Goldman was sent to prison for advocating that women need not always keep their mouths shut and their wombs open.'

As with Armand the headlines of Emma Goldman's campaign spoke louder than the contents and she was presumed to be an advocate of sexual licence. In fact there was an underlying modesty in her attitudes, a wish that people should love each other in a selfless fashion,

Top left: Emma Goldman whose public discussion of contraception was only one of her many stands against prejudice
Bottom left: Emile Armand who boldly asserted: 'Marriage is long-term prostitution; prostitution is short-term marriage.'
Left: Frank Wedekind, another leading German social dramatist

and when a Cincinatti brewer knocked at her hotel room thirsting for a night of free love she threatened to wake the whole hotel and expose him. It was the anarchist context of her campaign which rendered it immediately immoral to so many people, though the socialist Margaret Sanger who also launched the cause of birth control in the same years was treated in a similar way and fled from America in 1914 to avoid trial.

From Ferrer and Faure to Armand and Goldman, freedom from ignorance, superstition, and moral prejudice had been demanded in a direct confrontation with educational, religious, and moral authority. It was the main individualist method, the acting out of private convictions in the public arena of everyday life. But there were some anarchists who withdrew from society and made their own innovations in free living, as a detached and independent experiment.

Tolstoyan colonies were founded in the Russian provinces to develop the kind of communal, non-violent rural life which Tolstoy had portrayed as naturally good, and in 1890 a substantial number of Italian anarchists sailed to Brazil to found a New World colony dedicated to anarchist principles. Numbering over 200, the colonists were thwarted by the poverty of the land and their own internal disagreements, and the settlement, known as the Cecilia colony, collapsed after a few years. Like the Diggers of Cromwellian England the scheme appeared incurably romantic and utopian in retrospect, but the level of initial commitment was high and the intention serious.

The same can be said of smaller communities which were formed at the end of the century on the fringe of European society. Victor Serge visited one of these at Stockel in the Belgian forest of Soignes and in his memoirs gave an evocative picture of its idealism. On a small white house where the community lived was painted the slogan 'Do what you will' and at the entrance to the garden was a table with a pile of propaganda pamphlets and a saucer of small coins. Beside the saucer were written the words 'Take what you want, leave what you can.' Inside he found a speaker addressing a small group of listeners on the benefits of free love, though discussions of this kind did not impose any policy on the whole community. They were there to work and talk as they wanted, sharing all goods in common.

Both at Stockel and in other experiments of a similar nature, such as the community at Aiglemont in the

Right: 'Woman with Pillars' by Kees van Dongen. Although far from sympathetic with all aspects of anarchism, many artists identified with their demands for freedom for all individuals

Ardennes, this trust in honesty and generosity was not betrayed. What made the communities quickly impractical and caused their early collapse was the personal jealousy that developed among the members, often over sexual matters. This concentration on personal issues betrayed the absence of a specific economic function. Throughout the 19th century socialist thinkers of various descriptions had proposed the idea of workers' communities, but always with the proviso that they should be a viable economic unit of some kind. The small anarchist colonies in France and Belgium were not conceived as economic units and their freedom, however sincere, was no substitute for function. They were at best a spirited attempt to combine individual liberty and communal life, though many anarchists maintained that this could be done without withdrawing from society.

This was the belief of Albert Libertad, a destitute cripple who emerged in Paris in 1897 from an obscure provincial origin and became one of the most eloquent French defenders of individual freedom. In 1905 he founded the individualist journal *L'Anarchie* which called for an instant realisation of anarchist principles: 'Don't wait for the revolution, make your own by being free men and living in comradeship.' In the Parisian underworld, with little money and few illusions of a major social change, Libertad and his friends achieved something of this comradeship. But in the end their individualism divided as much as it united and Libertad himself resorted easily to force, using his crutches with considerable power to defend both his person and his ideas.

Freedom from orthodoxy

When anarchist communities of all kinds are considered, when the campaigns for educational freedom and moral independence are assessed, what appears constant among the many individualists involved is their readiness to experiment. Some undoubtedly had closed minds, and most were dogmatic in certain areas, but in general they were open to new ideas not only in the social and political fields but also in the realm of the arts. It was not that anarchism produced its own style of art or literature, nor that anarchists themselves were all great painters, writers or critics, but that their devotion to freedom brought them close to creative artists who were trying to free themselves from orthodoxy and tradition. Particularly in the art world of France it is difficult to discern where freedom ended and anarchy began.

Left: 'The Funeral Procession' by George Grosz. The horrors of the First World War and its aftermath were to force more and more artists to commit themselves totally to social reform

Camille Pissarro was one artist who blurred the distinction. As a leading Impressionist painter creating landscapes in which figures of peasants merge with their background into a composite rustic world of light, shadow, and colour, he was already under heavy criticism. Impressionism was greeted with derision by most of the critics and the fact that Pissarro was also anarchist in his ideas and was exiled for a short period after the Paris Commune, appeared to confirm, in the critics' eyes, their suspicion of his art. By the 1890s Impressionism was less of a novelty and Pissarro's paintings looked less revolutionary, but he continued to produce designs and drawings for anarchist publications and wrote of Kropotkin's *Conquest of Bread*: 'I must confess that, if it is utopian, it is in any case a very beautiful dream.'

Paul Signac was the other well-known anarchist artist in France, a painter who began the post-Impressionist experiment of building up his pictures by minuscule dots of colour which the eye at a distance formed into recognisable figures and objects. It was his belief that in the new society which anarchists were preparing, the ordinary man, the worker, would have the time and interest to appreciate art of all kinds, and he defined the anarchist painter as one who struggled 'with all his individuality, with a personal effort, against bourgeois and official conventions'.

In the anarchist periodicals started by Jean Grave, particularly *La Révolte,* these two artists and many other literary and artistic figures of the time like the poet Mallarmé, the painter Van Dongen, and the writer Alphonse Daudet, were represented by drawings, poems, or articles. Most of these artists were only occasional contributors and they were far from sympathetic to all kinds of anarchism, but they identified themselves with the freedom which the anarchists demanded for all individuals.

In England this anarchist freedom gained the enthusiasm of Oscar Wilde who signed a petition in favour of the Chicago anarchists, called for the abolition of property in order to free the individual, and in his book *The Soul of Man under Socialism* claimed that the artist and anarchist were identical in their demand for full individualism. Wilde flaunted convention by his dress, by his behaviour, and by his homosexuality for which he was legally prosecuted and socially ostracised: he had every personal as well as artistic reason to fight for the individual's freedom.

Right: A scene from Vigo's first film 'A propos de Nice' in which the director set out to portray 'the last gasps of society whose neglect of its responsibilities makes you sick'

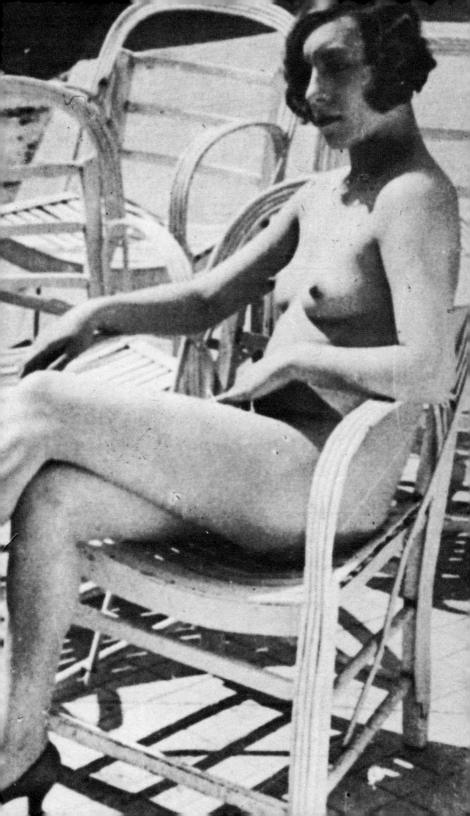

Wilde did not, however, carry conviction in all anarchist circles, for his final dedication was to art and the artist and he did not encourage the view that art should have a social purpose. For this reason his plays were not included in Emma Goldman's survey of contemporary drama in which she pointed to certain playwrights as powerful disseminators of radical thought. Her admiration went to Henrik Ibsen in particular: 'Ibsen, the supreme hater of all social shams, has torn the veil of hypocrisy from their faces.' Of his play *An Enemy of the People* she wrote 'In that great drama Ibsen performs the last funeral rites over a decaying and dying social system. Out of its ashes rises the regenerated individual, the bold and daring rebel.' The 'rebel' is Doctor Stockman who decides to reveal his discovery that the public baths of the town are built on a swamp and are therefore injurious to health. Financial interest, prejudice, and provincial pride coalesce against him and he is isolated. In Emma Goldman's words he finds his opponents 'a compact majority, unscrupulous enough to be willing to build up the prosperity of the town on a quagmire of lies and fraud'. She cannot speak too highly of this play, nor of *Ghosts,* which 'has acted like a bomb explosion, shaking the social structure to its very foundations'.

Her praise, in anarchist terms, also goes to the German playwrights Gerhardt Hauptmann and Frank Wedekind as well as to Bernard Shaw and to John Galsworthy, the latter for his play *Strife* which she held to be the most important labour play after Hauptmann's *Die Weber* (The Weavers). All these evaluations lead back to a long anarchist tradition, embodied in Proudhon, that art and literature should serve a social purpose and, although Emma Goldman was not blind to artistic merit, she clearly preferred literature which promoted social and individual freedom.

The anarchist cinema

To suggest this freedom was one of the aims of the celebrated film maker Jean Vigo, who was twelve when his anarchist father, known as Miguel Almereyda, was found strangled in a French police cell in 1917. Almereyda had been an anti-militarist before the war and became increasingly pacifist during it. Towards the middle of the war his social situation changed, he was seen to have money and property where before he was always on the verge of poverty. Had he become a traitor? Was he receiving German money for his pacifist writings? Was he strangled in a French prison for this reason? The answers are not known, but the young boy Jean Vigo believed his father to have been a model anarchist and revolutionary, and he inherited most of the views of the French anarchist

world in which Almereyda had been so prominent. In 1930 his film about Nice *(A propos de Nice)* expressed the anarchist's views on inequality. He compared the life of the rich, and the healthy, satisfied bodies of the suntanned holidaymakers, with the undernourished, deformed bodies of slum children, and in his comic film *Zéro de Conduite* (Nought for Conduct) his theme was a rebellion of schoolchildren against the rigidity of the school authorities. This was an explicit anarchist statement in which Vigo used anarchist friends as actors and it was immediately banned by the French authorities. Since then it has been recognised as a technical *tour de force* and stands as a source and precedent for the modern film by Lindsay Anderson, *If,* which portrays authority and rebellion in an English public school.

Of *A propos de Nice* Vigo stated, 'By displaying the atmosphere of Nice and the kind of lives lived down there — and, alas elsewhere — the film . . . [illustrates] the last gasps of a society whose neglect of its responsibilities makes you sick and drives you towards revolutionary solutions.' His own solutions remained shadowy for he died at the age of twenty-nine after completing his second major film *L'Atlante* which has a tenderly realised love relationship as its centre, though social criticism is also there with shots highlighting the misery of unemployed workers in Paris.

Vigo can be seen as a forceful exponent of his father's world, of the anarchist circles in pre-war Europe and America which were discussing not only revolution and inflammatory propaganda but also philosophy, poetry, and the art of the time. However slight, they formed a part of that cultural explosion at the beginning of the century which looked to freedom and experiment as its tools in the liberation of new forms, methods, and creative ideas.

Anarchism was not the only creed of freedom and to many contemporaries its destructive side seemed the very reverse of liberty, but without this aspect of creative innovation the history of anarchism would lack one of its vital dimensions. To freedom from ignorance, superstition, and moral prejudice one can justifiably add freedom from cultural orthodoxy, though the staunch campaigners for this freedom were only a minority in the anarchist ranks. Yet if anarchism is seen as a mosaic of richly coloured pieces, this piece, though smaller, was as richly coloured as the rest.

Left: *A shot from Vigo's last film 'L'Atalante' in which a tender love story is woven with social commentary on unemployment*

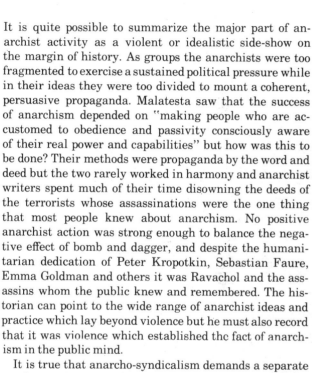

Conclusion
Myth and Reality

It is quite possible to summarize the major part of anarchist activity as a violent or idealistic side-show on the margin of history. As groups the anarchists were too fragmented to exercise a sustained political pressure while in their ideas they were too divided to mount a coherent, persuasive propaganda. Malatesta saw that the success of anarchism depended on "making people who are accustomed to obedience and passivity consciously aware of their real power and capabilities" but how was this to be done? Their methods were propaganda by the word and deed but the two rarely worked in harmony and anarchist writers spent much of their time disowning the deeds of the terrorists whose assassinations were the one thing that most people knew about anarchism. No positive anarchist action was strong enough to balance the negative effect of bomb and dagger, and despite the humanitarian dedication of Peter Kropotkin, Sebastian Faure, Emma Goldman and others it was Ravachol and the assassins whom the public knew and remembered. The historian can point to the wide range of anarchist ideas and practice which lay beyond violence but he must also record that it was violence which established the fact of anarchism in the public mind.

It is true that anarcho-syndicalism demands a separate conclusion. In trade union activity the uncompromising ideas of anarchy met the day to day needs of the working class and first in France and then in Spain a contribution was made to labour history which was more than marginal. In no country has the anarchist revolution arrived nor have the hopes placed in the General Strike been justified but for a generation of French and Spanish workers the mentality of revolutionary syndicalism ran deep.

But from the vantage point of to-day a summary in terms of success and failure accentuates the view that

Left: Despite the failure to change society, the ideals of anarchism have lived on to provide a focus for many who refuse to accept conventional authority. During the French revolts of 1968, anarchist-inspired parties played a leading role

anarchism lay outside the mainstream of events. Terror has brought terror and not freedom, revolutions in the 20th century have been socialist, communist, nationalist or fascist but not anarchist and, despite the regional appeal of anarcho-syndicalism, most workers in the modern industrialised states prefer limited strikes and bargaining to the idea of united economic revolt. The individualists, on the other hand, successfully anticipated certain aspects of subsequent history: in many countries there has been a substantial growth in religious, educational and moral freedom. This development, however, can mostly be ascribed to forces other than anarchism.

Beyond this balance-sheet of achievement what does the history of anarchism reveal? At one level the anarchists produced a body of social criticism which cannot easily be ignored. They pointed to abuses and injustices which they as groups or individuals discerned in their own societies. In Spain they placed their emphasis on the combined tyranny of church and state, in Russia on the centralised autocracy of Tsardom, in France, Italy and America on the hypocrisy of the bourgeois and the misery of the labouring classes. In towns the anarchists fought against industrial exploitation and slum poverty; in the countryside against landlord pressure and the unequal distribution of land.

The anarchist analysis of social evils was rooted in these realities. This was life as they themselves knew it. When they talked of prisons most of them talked on the basis of at least one prison sentence; when inveighed against the authority of Church and State most of them were victims of it; when they thundered against moral prejudice they knew the meaning of censorship and moral persecution. To this extent the anarchists worked from the raw material of life, the reality of their own experience. As a result there is much in anarchist writings which can serve the historian as useful documentation. The portrait of society which anarchists offered cannot be dismissed as mere propaganda. Most anarchists were actors and observers in the squalid world of the underprivileged; no one who wishes to understand that world can afford to neglect either their actions or their observations.

But there was more to anarchism than social analysis. There was the whole range of methods, expectations, assumptions, and ideals which separated anarchists from

Right: Continuing in the anarchist tradition of protest against the inadequacies of modern society, groups occupied empty buildings in London in 1969 or demonstrated in the streets (top right). Other groups chose to reject the conventional standards and values of Western society entirely (bottom right)

other social critics, whether liberal reformers or working-class socialists.

Did anarchists draw realistic lessons from their experiences or were their ideals lost in a world of myth and illusion? The anarchists were not unaware of this problem. They constantly defended themselves against the charge of utopian idealism and they criticised those in their own ranks who fell prey to unreality. The assassins were strongly criticised for trying to achieve vast social and political change by the single act of pistol or dagger, while the anarcho-syndicalists and the collective revolutionaries accused each other of false deductions and hopeless illusions.

From the outside it was not just one group of anarchists or another who were seen as dreamers. The whole concept of anarchy was held to be a myth. Socialists maintained it ignored economic realities and the historical role of the working class; liberals condemned it as impractical, and conservatives claimed that it flew in the face of natural inequalities and the human need for authority. In the 20th century revelations have come from psychology and sociology of man's aggressive nature and his competitiveness but also of his need for security. It has become a catchphrase that man is afraid of freedom, that he prefers to live and work within a settled, familiar structure. Sociologists have observed the rapidity with which groups produce leaders, and certain studies suggest that absence of authority weakens a group and jeopardises its chances of survival. Of course it is admitted that people want certain freedoms, freedom of movement, thought and speech, but do they want total freedom? The answer given by so many experts on human behaviour is no, and the failure of anarchism is held as evidence of this fact.

A minority attraction

Certainly the historian must agree that the ideal of anarchy was never a popular one, that it was opposed by people of all classes and all ages. It did not even become the creed of adolescent youth, the age group which is most naturally involved in problems of authority. There were young people, students, and others, among the anarchists, but there were more among socialists and still more among youth organisations of nationalist or religious convictions. The youth of Europe in 1900 had a capacity for following a strong lead and of ritualising the cult of the hero: anarchism was never more than a minority attraction.

But the anarchist hope lay less in the present than in the future, in the belief that man would one day grasp his freedom, would see that authority was a restriction

and not a necessity and would, by experience, discover that anarchy was a just and perfect solution to the human condition. This belief was, without doubt, a myth, but a myth in a different sense, in the sense used by the French philosopher Georges Sorel at the beginning of the 20th century. He claimed that a myth which lay in the future was an inspiration and a spur to action. The working classes, he stated, needed a myth to drive them on, to keep the light of revolution before their eyes, and he proposed the ideal of the General Strike which the anarcho-syndicalists had already adopted.

For the anarchists generally the ideal of anarchy, a society without government, was just such a myth. They prophesied its coming, they launched a thousand campaigns in favour of it, they killed and died for it. It is true that their methods and doctrine isolated them from their contemporaries but this trust in a future society brought them from the margin to the centre of history, for myths of the future abound in the history of the West. In particular Christianity and Marxism have produced myths with the same potency to lead and inspire. The anarchists have their vision of free and equal men, the Christians preach the kingdom of God on earth and the Marxists their classless socialist society. All three look different though they may be variants of the same ideal, and all three, as myths of the future, have the power of surviving past and present failures.

For this reason the final balance-sheet of anarchism, as of Christianity and Marxism, cannot yet be drawn. But of the anarchists of 1880-1914 the historian may well conclude that their propaganda by word and deed brought the myth of anarchy no nearer to reality.

Left: *Red Guards in China. Even in the most active and sweeping revolution of modern times, it became necessary to rekindle enthusiasm to totally rebuild society and reject former ideas*

121

Chronology of Events

1864 Marx launches the first International Working Men's Association at St Martin's Hall in London. In Italy, Mikhail Bakunin founds the International Brotherhood

1865 Pierre Joseph Proudhon, the father of anarchism, dies

1868 The third conference of the International is held at Brussels. **September:** Bakunin founds the International Social Democratic Alliance.

1869 **September:** a congress of the International is held at Basle.

1871 **Autumn:** the *Fédération Jurassienne* is founded under the influence of Bakunin, and headed by James Guillaume

1876 Bakunin dies (**1st July**). Prince Peter Kropotkin escapes from prison in St Petersburg and makes his way to Europe

1882 **22nd October:** Cyvogt is imprisoned for life after a bomb is planted in the Bellecour Theatre at Lyon

1886 **4th May:** a bomb is thrown in Haymarket Square, Chicago **11th November:** four anarchists are hanged although their guilt is not proven

1892 Emma Goldman supports Alexander Berkman in an unsuccessful attempt to assassinate Henry Clay Frick in Homestead, Pennsylvania, after a lock-out at the Carnegie Corporation's works **March:** Ravachol plants bombs in the Boulevard St Germain (11th) and the Rue de Clichy (27th) **25th April:** on the eve of his trial, the Restaurant Véry is blown up with its proprietor who informed on Ravachol. Ravachol is guillotined

1893 **24th September:** at Barcelona, Pallás throws a bomb at General Martinez Campos, killing him. Pallás is garrotted **8th November:** a bomb is thrown in the Teatro Liceo by Santiago Salvador to avenge Pallás. **9th December:** in Paris, Vaillant throws a bomb into the Chamber of Deputies. He is guillotined **11th December:** criminal laws are voted intensifying anti-anarchist repression

1894 **12th February:** in Paris Emile Henry throws a bomb at the Terminus-St-Lazare. He is guillotined **24th June:** President Sadi-Carnot is assassinated by Santo Jeronimo Caserio, an Italian anarchist, at Lyon

1895 Pelloutier becomes secretary of the *Fédération des Bourses du Travail*. At Limoges the *Confédération generale du Travail* is founded

1897 Cánovas del Castillo, the Spanish prime minister, is assassinated by Angiolillo, in revenge for Montjuich

1898 Empress Elizabeth of Austria-Hungary is assassinated by an Italian anarchist on the shores of Lake Geneva

1900 **July:** King Umberto I is assassinated at Monza by Bresci

1906 The CGT hold a congress at Amiens. The Charter of Amiens is adopted, reaffirming syndicalist principles

1907 An international congress of anarchists is held at Amsterdam and Monatte and Malatesta hold opposing views on the linking of anarchism with syndicalism

1909 **July:** *Semana Trágica* — riots take place in Barcelona **13th October:** Francisco Ferrer, founder of the *Escuela Moderna*, is shot for his alleged participation

1912 **12th November:** Canalejas y Mendez, prime minister of Spain, is assassinated in Madrid by an anarchist

Top: Pierre Ramus, leader of French anarchism between the wars (left). The cover of Kropotkin's Temps Nouveaux (middle). A barricade during the Paris Commune (right). **Centre:** Militia drilling during the Spanish civil war (left). An allegory on the plight of the workers from 'l'Almanach de Pere Renard' (middle). The assassination of Tsar Alexander II (right). **Bottom:** Member of a California hippy colony (left). A poster for Ubu Roi (centre). A scene from L'Age d'Or (right)

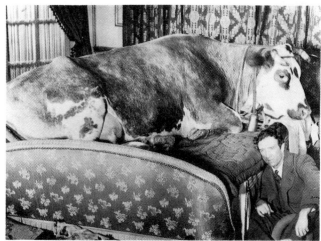

Index of main people, places, and events

Author's suggestions for further reading

The most comprehensive survey of both the ideas and the actions of the anarchists is found in George Woodcock's *Anarchism* (1962) and James Joll's *The Anarchists* (1964). Together they provide scholarly information and perceptive insights and, although they duplicate each other in several ways, their distinctive qualities emerge. Both contain a good deal of quotation from anarchist writings but for longer extracts one turns to *Patterns of Anarchy* edited by Leonard I. Krimerman and Lewis Perry (1966) which has a highly interesting selection, and to *The Anarchists* edited by Irving L. Horowitz (1964) whose introductory essay is a model of lucidity.

For more specialised information, country by country, there are several excellent treatments. For France Jean Maitron's *Histoire du mouvement anarchiste en France 1880-1914* (1955) was a pioneer study of great importance. For Russia there is Paul Avrich's *The Russian Anarchists* (1967) which is full of detail and for Spain there are two studies which capture brilliantly the atmosphere of Spanish anarchism, Gerald Brenan's *The Spanish Labyrinth* (First edition 1943) and E.J.Hobsbawn's *Primitive Rebels* 1959 (chapter on 'The Andalusian Anarchists').

Individuals are served by *The Anarchist Prince, A biography of Peter Kropotkin* by George Woodcock and Ivan Avakumović (1950), Richard Drinnon's *Rebel in Paradise, A biography of Emma Goldman* (1961) and *Errico Malatesta, His Life and Ideas* edited by Vernon Richards.

Perhaps the most authentic approach is to watch for the various reprints of anarchist pamphlets and speeches, which anarchist groups continue to publish in several countries. In England The Freedom Press have done much in this way to make original sources available to a wide public.

Library of the 20th Century will include the following titles:

Russia in Revolt
David Floyd
The Second Reich
Harold Kurtz
The Anarchists
Roderick Kedward
Suffragettes International
Trevor Lloyd
War by Time-Table
A.J.P.Taylor
Death of a Generation
Alistair Horne
Suicide of the Empires
Alan Clark
Twilight of the Habsburgs
Z.A.B.Zeman
Early Aviation
Sir Robert Saundby
Birth of the Movies
D.J.Wenden
Theodore Roosevelt
A.E.Campbell
Lenin's Russia
G.Katkov
The Weimar Republic
Sefton Delmer
Out of the Lion's Paw
Constantine Fitzgibbon
Japan: The Years of Triumph
Louis Allen
Communism Takes China
C.P.Fitzgerald
Black and White in South Africa
G.H.Le May
Woodrow Wilson
R.H.Ferrell
France 1918-34
W.Knapp
France 1934-40
A.N.Wahl
Mussolini's Italy
Geoffrey Warner
The Little Dictators
A.Polonsky
Viva Zapata
L.Bethell
The World Depression
Malcolm Falkus
Stalin's Russia
A.Nova
The Brutal Reich
Donald Watt
The Spanish Civil War
Raymond Carr
Munich: Czech Tragedy
K.G.Robbins

HR Kedward is Lecturer in European History at the University of Sussex. His previous books are *The Dreyfus Affair* (1965) and *Fascism in Western Europe* (1969). In 1968-69 he held a Leverhulme Fellowship for research into French Resistance.

JM Roberts, General Editor of the *Macdonald Library of the 20th Century,* is Fellow and Tutor in Modern History at Merton College, Oxford. He is also General Editor of Purnell's *History of the 20th Century* and Joint-Editor of the *English Historical Review,* and author of *Europe 1880-1945* in the Longman's History of Europe. He has been English Editor of the *Larousse Encyclopedia of Modern History,* has reviewed for *The Observer, New Statesman,* and *Spectator,* and given talks on the BBC

Library of the 20th Century

Publisher: Iain Sproat
Editor: Jonathan Martin
Executive Editor: Richard Johnson
Assistant Editor: Jenny Ashby
Designed by: Brian Mayers/ Germano Facetti
Design: Henning Boehlke
Research: John Deakin

Pictures selected from the following sources:

Assiette au Beurre 69
Bertarelli, Milan 77
Bibliothèque Nationale, Paris 70
Camera Press Ltd 120
Collection Sirot 57
Flavio Costantini 4 15 37 66
Culver Picture Library 87
Gallery of Modern Art, Milan 98
Gernsheim Collection, University of Texas 8 52
Greater London Council Photo Library 8 84
Estate of George Grosz 110
Harlingue-Viollet 78
John Heartfield 97
Holmes-Lebel, Paris 119
Instituto Municipal de Historia, Barcelona 60 64
International Institute of Social History, Amsterdam 87 106
Billy Jay 97
Le Petit Journal 34 43 44
Le Rire 72-3
L'Illustration 51 62 64 69
L'Illustration/Bradford City Library 90
Mansell Collection 8 10 18 19 31 40 88
Marlborough Fine Art (London) Ltd 101 102 109
Museo d'Arte Moderna, Milan 74
National Film Archive 96 113 114
Novosti 80
Paul Popper 96 119
Punch 23
Radio Times Hulton Picture Library 10 26 27 29 92 94 106
Roger-Viollet 20 25 82 87
Simplicissimus 69
Snark 7 10 12 16 20 25 26 27 38 40 47 49 55 57 72-3 116
Snark/Ringart 27 49
Staatsbibliothek, Berlin 106
Südd-Verlag, Munich 119
Hans Tasiemka 58
Ullstein 104
World of Atget (Horizon Press) Berenice Abbott 32

LA COMPLAINTE DE VAILLANT

OU L'ATTENTAT DE LA CHAMBRE DES DÉPUTÉS

Paroles de
F. XAN-NEUF

Musique de
ÉMILE SPENCER

LIBRAIRIE POPULAIRE, 26, Rue Tiquetonne, PARIS